LOWESTOFT
PEOPLE & PLACES

IAN G. ROBB

The
History
Press

The History Press
The Mill • Brimscombe Port • Stroud •
Gloucestershire • GL5 2QG

First published 2009
Reprinted 2014

Copyright © Ian G. Robb, 2009

British Library Cataloguing in Publication Data
A catalogue record for this book is available from the
British Library.

ISBN 978-07509-2416-0

Typeset in 10.5/13.5 Photina.
Typesetting and origination by
The History Press.
Printed and bound in Great Britain by
Marston Book Services Limited, Oxfordshire

E.E. Cooper, *The Gondoliers*, 1926. Gilbert and Sullivan operas were immensely popular with audiences in Lowestoft before and after the First World War. Mr Cooper was also the secretary of the Lowestoft Gilbert and Sullivan Opera Club, a rival to the Lowestoft Amateur Operatic and Dramatic Society.

CONTENTS

Waiting for the swing bridge, Pier Terrace, c. 1909. Lowestoft's trams had entered service in 1903 and this particular type of tramcar, one of two types used in the town, was usually for summer use. The Glendower Restaurant later became the Glendower Bakery. The 'her' (upper left) marks Henry Jenkins' photographic studio at 2 Pier Terrace. The swing bridge was replaced in 1972 by the present bascule bridge.

INTRODUCTION

With the exception of two world wars, Lowestoft's history has been one of growth. The resort, the fishing, and industries such as shipbuilding and engineering, all attracted people to the town and made Lowestoft's name internationally renown. Sir Morton Peto's vision of Lowestoft fish reaching inland markets by railway within twenty-four hours of landing, and a health resort based on a new site south of the ancient town, went far beyond the dreams of anyone who attended that fateful meeting in 1844 at Peto's residence at Somerleyton Hall.

Sir Morton Peto's arrival saw Lowestoft grow at such a rate that by the census of 1891 it had become the second largest town in Suffolk, a position it still holds today. Its fame drew in men such as John Walter Brooke and Samuel Richards, both who eventually set up businesses that became household names in their own right. The fishing also attracted the Scots, not just the drifters or the girls working on the pickling plots, but entrepreneurs such as the Maconochie brothers, or Charles and Edward Morton, who set up fish processing factories on the South Quay. Such were the sheer numbers of jobs to be found in the town, that even as late as the 1970s in some parts of Lowestoft one could literally walk across the road from one job into another. Today, of course, everything is very different. Only one significant food processing factory, Birds Eye, opened in 1949, survives; the shipyards have gone, as have the coachworks, and what is left of the fishing industry is but a microcosm of its former self.

A book about Lowestoft is also a book about its people; those who worked, lived and played here. To service his new town, Peto created what could be said to be the first artisan estate in Lowestoft. Built for his labourers working on the railway, the New Town Estate and the Fish Market, Bevan Street (now Bevan Street West) and Tonning Street were also the first large-scale 'social housing' in Lowestoft. Coupled with the north side of Commercial Road, these two streets are now all too rare examples of Peto's industrial heritage in the town.

Music and music-making have always played an important part in local life. Before the days of radio and television, people made their own entertainment, occasionally forming a musical or dramatic society or club. Lowestoft's own interest in Gilbert and Sullivan stems back to the palmy days of the late 1890s and HMS *Hearty*. This interest in drama and the arts in turn attracted professional actors and actresses of the calibre of Hayden Coffin and Irene Vanbrugh to the town. Even today with the Lowestoft Players, there is still a lively interest in amateur theatricals. As to music, it is with some pride that the Royal Philharmonic Orchestra has been Lowestoft's resident orchestra for some years.

'The war' – that is the Second World War – is still with us. The town centre took over forty years to recover, with the Britten Centre, which opened in 1987, finally replacing the Victoria Arcade which was destroyed in 1941. Throughout this book I still through force of habit refer to the 1939–45 period as 'the war' or 'the last war', phrases my parents and my grandparents also used.

Life may have altered radically over the postwar years, particularly in the last twenty years, but Lowestoft's bridge, or I should say more correctly, Lowestoft's Bridge, maintains its influence over daily life on both sides of Lake Lothing. The first two bridges were built when the port's commercial traffic travelled extensively by sea; even after the arrival of the railway in 1847 and into the twentieth century, the North Sea continued to act as a major trading route. This changed in the postwar years when commercial road transport finally superseded both sea and rail. The swing bridge built in 1897 only had two lanes; even so, the present bascule bridge opened in 1972 also started life with two lanes! Although changed later to three lanes, it still remains inadequate for the number of vehicles travelling over the river today. The crossing even created a new word in the English language, 'Bridger'; a one-word phrase which for a century and more has described the reason for lateness, missed appointments, missed buses, the length of traffic queues, et cetera. The term is believed to have originated in the days of sail when fishing vessels had priority over road transport.

Of all the changes that have taken place over the last twenty years, it was the speed in which Lowestoft lost the majority of its major employers and in a such short time. Mortons, which closed in 1988, was followed by Brooke Yachts in 1993 (Brooke Marine had changed its name in 1988); after being taken over by Barber Richmore, the number one Co-op factory closed in 1994, the same year also saw the demise of Richards. The Co-op number two factory closed in 1997. North Lowestoft was not left out – the prestigious Eastern Coachworks closed in 1988, followed by Bally Shoes two years later. Such a dramatic loss of employment and all within a space of ten years had, and still has, a devastating effect on the town. But more was to follow, eclipsing all with the passing of the last of Lowestoft's deep sea fishing fleet in 2003.

Lowestoft has a reputation of bouncing back, however. The conclusion of the Waveney Sunrise Scheme saw the return of Kirkley as the centre of Lowestoft's South Beach holiday resort, although the lack of easily accessible car parks from the new South Lowestoft spine road to the resort have caused some teething problems, and already Lowestoft has made inroads as a pioneer in renewable energies, spearheaded by 'Gulliver' built in 2004 as the largest on-shore wind turbine in the country.

Ian G. Robb, 2009

1

The High Street &
the Old Town Area

Triangle Market, High Street, c. 1993. It is obvious by the state of the stall roofs that sad times had reached the Triangle Market. Its days were indeed numbered, and in early 1996 the stalls were demolished. In the background is 88 High Street, indicated by the middle window, and the entrance to Maltsters Score. Lorenzo's Restaurant is on the right. (*Author*)

High Street, Lowestoft, *c*. 1896. One of a series taken by Charles Metcalf of the upper High Street prior to its demolition, this part of the street was one of the narrowest in the old town. The Star of Hope, on the corner of Compass Lane, was one of a number of public houses clustered round the Town Hall and had been open for approximately forty years. Its Victorian façade replaced a jettied timber-framed Tudor building; the Town Hall entrance is marked by the large building, centre left, next to the trio of young mothers heavily wrapped up against the winter cold. It was built in 1857 on the site of the old Town Chamber and Corn Cross, itself constructed in 1698. Both the Town Chamber, and later the Town Hall, were used for concerts by visiting artistes or played host to curiosities such as the American Tom Thumb during his visit to Norfolk and Suffolk in 1844. Everything on the left was demolished in the 1890s. The front of the Town Hall was moved back 15ft and subsequently enlarged between 1900 and 1904. Most of the buildings on the cliff side, on the right of the photograph, still survive. Apart from the Sea View Temperance Hotel and the shop next door, this side of the High Street remains much the same today. The shop to the right of the stationary horse and cart, then Thirtles the ironmongers, was originally Chaston House. George II rested here in January 1737 after a very rough sea journey across the North Sea from Germany.

Many of the surviving houses retain traces of their earlier history; however, several of those seen in the background had a narrow escape in November 2004, when the derelict Ashley Boys' Club nearby in Mariners Score was destroyed by a fire which threatened to engulf some of the houses in the High Street.

Belle Vue Park, *c.* 1885. Once the town's drying ground, a park had been proposed here as early as the 1830s. The park was eventually opened in 1874 and is seen here from North Parade in its early finery. The fountain at the foot of the spiral steps was fed by a natural spring. The pagoda-style bandstand was replaced in 1953 by the Royal Naval Patrol Service Memorial.

The interior of 30 High Street, *c.* 1908. This was the home of William Hallam, solicitor and member of the Borough's Public Library committee until his death in 1915. The seventeenth-century fireplace has delftware tiles on each side of a late eighteenth-century grating. Note the gas lighting (top left), the early portraits, and two lethal-looking crossbows on the mantelpiece!

St Margaret's Church and the area around Church Road, December 1992. The view was taken from the rooftop of St Peter's Court, Lowestoft's one and only high-rise, well before today's collection of microwave aerials made it too dangerous. Looking towards St Margaret's church, it is a rare opportunity to observe over a thousand years of Lowestoft's history all in one go. The area beyond the church was once the manor of Akethorpe and mentioned in the Domesday Book; the road travelling diagonally from the bottom right to the left of the photograph, today's Crown Street West, was at one time the main coach road into the old town from Mutford Bridge (now Oulton Broad). St Margaret's Church, enlarged in the 1480s, stands on the highest point in north Lowestoft. Church Road, the other road travelling diagonally, and seen here on the extreme right with bay-windowed houses, may be the oldest road in north Lowestoft. Originally linking the small medieval community around the church to the cliffs and the North Denes, until the early 1960s when the flats in the Hemplands were built across its path, Church Road wound itself from St Margaret's into Mariners Street, across the High Street and down Mariners Score onto the Denes. Most of the houses surrounding St Peter's Court date from the 1860s onwards, but most here are mainly due to twentieth-century expansion. To the left of St Margaret's is the Waveney Sports Centre in Water Lane, an area once marshland and is the reason why Church Road tends to weave its way erratically towards the High Street at this point. Touching the horizon is the white castellated water tower in Hollingsworth Road. (*Author*)

Masons Bakery, 58 High Street, 1981. Founded by D.R. Mason, his first shop here was in the wrecked shell of the International Stores, which was bombed in February 1941. A new shop was commissioned in 1958. Following his retirement in the 1970s, the business was sold to a Mr Heil, a baker from Surrey, and would later become a branch of Heils Bakery in London Road North. (*Ken Carsey*)

Masons Bakery, Gordon Road, *c.* 1982. At one time Masons boasted two other branches – one in London Road South and this small shop only yards away from the noise and bustle of London Road North. Built, I believe, in the 1970s, it looks so out of place in front of the plain wall of the Tesco supermarket. Despite its location, it survived some twenty years before closing. (*Ken Carsey*)

The Triangle Market on the corner of the High Street and St Peter's Street, *c.* 1981. The market had originally moved to this, supposedly temporary site, in the 1890s. The location proved popular with the townspeople and it remained here for the next hundred years! It sold fruit, vegetables, clothes, second-hand goods; in fact everything you needed and all in one spot.

The large dark building with the advertising hoarding is still remembered as Devereux's, a grocery business that survived into the 1970s; the modern CMC warehouse was built for Devereux's not long before they closed. To the right is the High Street, complete with buildings that go back half a millennium. Many are Tudor dwellings built on medieval foundations.

An application had been made for a market as early as 1308, although its location is now uncertain. However, a market was held at Old Market Plain from 1442 to 1698 when it moved to the Corn Cross. There it stayed until 1856, gradually expanding until the building of the town hall, when it moved to the New Market Plain opposite in Compass Lane. The Triangle Market was pleasant in summer, but its location unfortunately meant it was bitterly cold during the winter. Despite surviving two world wars, the movement of businesses into London Road North in the 1950s, and although slightly affected by the opening of the Britten Centre market in the late 1980s, it was the construction of Artillery Way in 1994, separating the High Street from London Road North, that led to its demise. The present-day Triangle Market, although a shadow of its former self, remains popular. (*Ken Carsey*)

Mrs Seago's Dairy, 38 Mariners
Street, *c.* 1958. Small shops could
once be found everywhere. The
mainstay of their community,
every side street it seemed had
at least one dealing in some
commodity or another. The dairy,
located in what may have been
one of the oldest thoroughfares in
Lowestoft, followed a tradition that
went back centuries. The shop was
demolished in November 1958.

The Kandy Kabin, 84 High
Street, 1930s. William Uridge's
sweet shop had a window
crammed full of sweets,
chocolates and cigarettes.
Picture postcards and saucy
seaside postcards made up the
rest of the trade. Situated next
to Parker & Watson (right)
whose shop was destroyed in
the last war, it continued as a
confectioners until 1960 when it
became G. & B. Thacker's sewing
machine shop.

The Triangle, St Peter's Street, summer 1993. The High Street is in the background with the Triangle Market Place on the left. Taken not long before the opening of Artillery Way in 1994, a visiting bus from Barking, Essex, passes Taylor's antique shop on the right, which became the Lowestoft Arts Centre in 2001. Until 1962 the tall building, centre left, was the London Drapery Stores. (*Author*)

Nos 51 to 53 High Street, *c.* 1980. Howes Video (centre) at no. 51, was originally the Lion, one of the many public houses and inns in this part of seventeenth- and eighteenth-century Lowestoft. There has been a shop here since 1768 and the days of the town's first resort. It became a branch of Matthes Bakery in 1953, closing in the mid-1970s. Heiner of Switzerland were at 52 High Street from 1977 to 2000. Heiner Leuenberger himself actually came from Switzerland; the business was taken over by Stephen and Margaret Cowell opening as Rise Hairdressers in 2000. North Lowestoft Post Office, next door at 53 High Street, moved from no. 140, on the opposite side of the street, in 1932. Like many premises on the cliff side, the post office suffered damage during the war. A new front was built by 1952; this was subsequently rebuilt in the 1990s. Beyond Crown Score and Howes Video, nos 49a and 50a High Street are covered by scaffolding. (*Ken Carsey*)

Opposite, bottom: Christmas bridal show, London Drapery Stores, 95–8 High Street, 1930s. Obviously looking forward to traditional spring weddings as well as fashions for the forthcoming season, the tree in the right-hand corner is the only clue as to the time of year. Wrapped in furs, everyone in the audience and on the catwalk is female. Is it possible the live mannequins were London Drapery Stores staff?

High Street, *c.* 1981. Nearest to the camera is Lawrence Green, gentlemen's tailor, with fellow outfitter David King next door. North End Fish Stores, run for many years by Brian Pull, is on the other side of the alleyway leading to the Scout headquarters at the rear. Looking towards the Triangle, the southern part of the High Street become pedestrian prioritised in the late 1990s. (*Ken Carsey*)

High Street, *c.* 1896. This part of the High Street was once irreverently called by Adam Adams, one of the town's early mayors, the 'fag end of Lowestoft'. However, what was here was some five hundred years of the town's development. As with other parts of the High Street, houses and shops were built on late medieval foundations, and like other parts of the old town, Tudor façades and interiors were hidden away by later, more modern frontages. The street was widened in 1897 and all of those on the left-hand side, the western side of the street, demolished. G.J. Cook, bakers and grocers (left, complete with Hudson's Soap enamel sign), is tucked between an eighteenth-century house and a Dutch gable belonging to a seventeenth-century property. To the right of the young girl with the infants is the original Three Herring public house, later to move to a temporary site opposite Arnold House before finally reopening in 1903 on the corner of St Margaret's Road as the Belle Vue.

The rectory, the tall building nearest to the camera on the right-hand side of the street, the cliff side, was nearly thirty years old when this photograph was taken and is the only contemporary building on either side of the street. The large house in the distance on the same side of the street is Arnold House, built the previous century and until 1901 the home of Mrs Arnold, the last of the Arnold family at Lowestoft. All the buildings on the right closest to the camera survived up to the evening of 12 May 1943, when they were destroyed in the Fokker-Wulf raid on the High Street.

Opposite, bottom: Fillingham's, 59 High Street, c. 1980. A chemist's shop has been here since the 1840s. Run by Edwin Corkhill from the 1920s to the late 1950s, it still retains much of its early Victorian frontage. The interior also reflects its long history as a chemists, and is complete with original fittings and a painting of the arms of the Worshipful Company of Apothecaries. (*Ken Carsey*)

Coopers Warehouse on the corner of White Horse Street and Compass Street, 1984. Then a grocery warehouse, it faced Jubilee Way, which had been built in 1977 through the Hemplands and much of White Horse Street. The prefabricated building on the right is on the site of the White Horse public house. At the time of writing, both buildings house Waveney District Council offices. (*Author*)

Water Lane Stores, *c.* 1920. The off-licence was built on the side of 29 Water Lane. Standing in the doorway is James William Alger, who ran the premises from 1901 or 1902 to 1930 when it was taken over by Bernard Dyer. In existence at the outbreak of war in 1939, it appeared not to have survived and may have been destroyed during the raid on the town on 18 March 1943.

North Flint House, High Street, *c.* 1950. Built in the mid-sixteenth century, the house was the temporary home of Lowestoft's public library following its destruction in Clapham Road by bombing in March 1941. It remained here until 1951 when it moved to Suffolk Road. The house then became Lowestoft Corporation's housing department. To the left are the ruins of the Candy Store wrecked in May 1943.

James Kirby Alger in his upholstery workshop, St Peter's Street, *c.* 1951. Another member of the prolific Alger family, James had a workshop opposite Thurston Road in 1926. By 1950, he had moved to 242 St Peter's Street, not far from Water Lane and had retired by 1958. The family also had an interest in Oxford Road as haulage contractors and fertiliser merchants.

Lowestoft Volunteer Training Corps, 1914. The two women on the left look on light-heartedly as members of the local corps – which included one tall hatless youth – make their way past the New Drill Hall in Beccles Road (now part of St Peter's Street), towards Beresford Road. It's worth speculating just how many of these men came back from the front in 1918.

Kent Road, Lowestoft bombardment, 25 April 1916. In the early hours of Tuesday morning a German battleship squadron opened fire on the town. Although four people were killed, there were several close calls, caused mainly by shells not exploding. One such near-miss occurred in Kent Road when a shell ploughed through a terrace of thirteen houses without exploding or killing anyone.

Lowestoft Corporation smithy, *c. 1938*. At one time there were several smithies in the town. One, Thirtles, was at Old Market Plain, this one, the Borough smithy, was down in Rotterdam Road. Once, almost everything needed for the borough of Lowestoft – from road signs, park signs, to metalwork and wooden fixtures, possibly even horseshoes – were all made at the borough workshops. The site also contained the Borough's electricity station, located on the corner of Norwich Road. In the days before health and safety, and vastly different from today's Waveney District Council workshops on the same site, the Borough blacksmiths pose here over their forges in their workshop at Smith's Marsh, Rotterdam Road. The photographer later added the sparks from the acetylene torch.

The photograph itself is somewhat of a rarity, taken between January 1936 and June 1939 for the *Lowestoft Mercury*, in its day a serious rival to the *Lowestoft Journal*. The *Mercury* considered itself a 'people's newspaper', but disappeared at the outbreak of war in September 1939.

Barclays Bank, High Street, 1991. I find it hard to believe this was built as one of Lowestoft's coaching inns – the Star Hotel. Gurney's Bank took over the premises in the mid-1850s before becoming part of Barclays Bank by the end of the century. After 140 years of sterling service, it finally closed its doors not long after this photograph was taken. The single-storey building on the left housed the bank's vaults, now, of course, long removed! Today, the bank is now Bank House, a private residence.

To the right of the bank, and at the time almost derelict, is Holm View, the once-grand home of William Youngman, Lowestoft's largest brewer and in 1885 its first mayor. Youngman also owned several properties to the right of the house and up to the corner of Rant Score; the taller block was built in the 1890s on the site of three earlier shops, one which retained its eighteenth-century bay-fronted window to the end. In the 1920s Holm View was a girl's college run by a mother superior before becoming Lowestoft Secretarial College in the 1950s. Despite being host to a variety of other businesses, the house eventually became empty and dilapidated for some years. In November 1993 two of its ornate fireplaces were stolen. In more recent years it has been turned into flats. (*Author*)

2

London Road North & the Surrounding Area

A Wayland bus waits outside Tesco's London Road North, 1992. This bus stop
superseded the Arcade stop further up the road outside the Lowestoft Journal office. After
deregulation, companies including Wayland's began expanding their services to outlying
towns such as Southwold (misspelled here as South Wold) and Halesworth. The bus is a
Cresta-bodied Range Rover. (*Author*)

Nos 95 and 97 London Road North, *c.* 1900. Stuarts Ltd at no. 95, behind the lamppost, specialised in sports outfits for the gentleman visitor. Popular were tennis and football, and for the really well-to-do, shooting and golf. Next door at no. 97, the larger of the two shops, Fredyric W. Bryant, ladies' tailor and outfitter would show the mistress of the house the latest styles and fashions. The two shops faced the Marina.

In the 1860s, London Road, as it was then known, consisted mainly of the homes of the wealthy and successful physicians. As the town rapidly grew, shops gradually took over the gardens of some of these houses, two of which can be seen behind nos 95 and 97. The splitting up of the Grove estate into building plots also speeded up the change from a residential thoroughfare to what would eventually become the town centre. By the early 1920s both shops had been taken over by Arnolds. They and the houses behind them were demolished in 1933 and a new store was built for Universal Stores.

BHS, 95–7 London Road North, *c.* 1985. Originally built for Universal Stores, the store was wrecked in the Waller Raid of 1942. Reopened after the war as a branch of British Home Stores, it is seen here in its later guise as BHS at the start of the town centre pedestrian precinct. The entrance to the Prairie further down on the same side marks the Britten Centre, then under construction. (*Ken Carsey*)

Universal Stores staff on the roof of 95–7 London Road North, c. 1936. No self-service then; it was an era of smart department stores with well-stocked counters and customers served personally by well-dressed shop assistants. The five men seem to be somewhat apprehensive sitting among so many young ladies! The average wage for these girls was reported to be around 12*s* 6*d* a week.

Denmark Road, April 1915. The first Zeppelin raids on the town took place in April 1915. Although the bombs were small and dropped by hand, they still caused considerable damage. One hit the tram lines outside the Central railway station which were coated with a coloured liquid that remained warm to the touch for thirty minutes.

R. & L. Latten's timber yard, Commercial Road, April 1915. Although the target appeared to be the railway, the first bomb actually landed on Latten's yard, killing a horse. The attack also included Denmark Road and Bevan Street where shops had their windows wrecked by bomb blast.

The Swing Bridge and Inner Harbour, c. 1938. Two drifters pass through the bridge in the final months of peace. Air-raid precautions had been augmented earlier that year and already there are signs of preparations for the inevitable conflict, noticeably the sandbags piled in front of the bridge-house (right). The harbour-master's house is the tall ornate building centre right.

Lowestoft Harbour works fire service, c. 1941. On 7 February 1941, a single raider dropped twenty bombs in an attempt to put the swing bridge out of action and cut the town in half. The bombs missed the bridge but destroyed the engine house and the harbour master's house. Ten men were killed and 37 injured. The crew here were responsible for digging for survivors following the raid.

London Road North and Waveney Road, 1985. A general view looking towards north Lowestoft and the town centre as seen from the Yacht Basin on the south side of the Bridge. Behind the bridge control house on the left is Commercial Road. The grand façade of Bambers store (centre right) marks the corner of London Road North and Waveney Road. To the immediate left of Bambers, Denmark Road and the entrance to Bevan Street can be seen in the distance. The offices of Hobsons and Small and Co. in Waveney Road overlook the Trawl Dock and face the Yacht Basin. In the Yacht Basin itself, among the yachts and small boats is the *Frederick Edward Crick*, the Lowestoft lifeboat from 1963 to 1987. The Colne Group rescue vessel is moored next to the RNLI lifeboat. To the left, and moored nearby is, if I recall, an experimental self-righting rescue craft. Already the well-known Lowestoft trawler was fast disappearing, the Trawl Basin is not so busy as it was only a decade before. (*Author*)

Station Square, London Road North, 1981. Walker-Regis is on the corner of Commercial Road, which until 1964 had been Barclays Bank. Janes, the premises with the verandah, was originally Dagmar House, built for J.R. O'Driscoll as a single-storey premises. Following the success of his various enterprises there, including a domestic servants' agency, it was enlarged to its present height by 1898. (*Ken Carsey*)

Station Square, London Road North, *c.* 1985. Walker-Regis remained on the corner of Commercial Road, however, James had now given way to a branch of Brahams, a department store founded in Great Yarmouth by Fay Braham before becoming a newsagent for a short period in the 1990s. (*Ken Carsey*)

The Bridge, Station Square, London Road North, *c. 1983*. The southern end of Station Square, Ford Jenkins moved his father's studio to 11 Station Square in 1955; the single-storey shops to the right of the terrace included Frederick Norton who was a tobacconists here from 1892 to the 1980s. The entrance to the yard next door also marks the junction of Commercial Road (right). (*Ken Carsey*)

Charrington's coal office, 5 Station Square, London Road North, 1982. The most interesting part of this small building was its ornate wooden door, which, according to local legend, came from a gentleman's residence. It is believed to have been transferred to the Lowestoft Heritage Workshop Centre after the building's demolition in 2004. (*Ken Carsey*)

Bambers department store, Station Square, *c.* 1982. Best remembered as Tuttles, the store covered the whole block from Suffolk Road on the left, to the junction of Waveney Road on the right. Tuttle's 'Bon Marché' emporium on the corner of Suffolk Road was one of the first to be constructed on the old Grove estate following its split into plots in 1885. Built for Ebeneezer Tuttle in 1888, in its time it was one of the most prestigious shops in the town. The building on the junction with Waveney Road, which is still called Tuttle's Corner today, and which is remembered for the fire that destroyed the turret in July 1964, was built in 1891 for Frederick Savage, the famous King's Lynn engineer, who also had family connections with Lowestoft. His initials, 'FS', can still be seen on the building between the first and second floors. Originally designed as a fish merchants, in 1892, it was being run as a family butcher by C. Burton. It became Savage & Son, a fellow butchers, until 1902, before becoming a bank and later Tuttles furniture galleries. It is also one of only three buildings left in north Lowestoft still displaying the original Borough of Lowestoft coat of arms.

Debenhams took over the running of the store in the 1960s, by which time it had expanded to cover almost the whole block. Tuttles closed its doors in July 1981; after a short period as Bambers and later as Ryans, the ground floor was turned into small shopping units. The square in front of the building formed the southern end of the London Road North pedestrian precinct in 1983. The car travelling past the camera is a Ford Capri. (*Ken Carsey*)

W.H. Smith kiosk, Lowestoft Central station, 1922. An important port of call for anyone coming off the train or for that something to read on a long journey; magazines, maps and postcards were always available, as were the latest guides to the resort. H.R. Prince took over the kiosk not long after Smith's opened their shop in London Road North in 1980. The timetable on the left hides the gents' toilets.

Lowestoft Central station, 1979. Looking towards the booking hall in the days of British Rail; in the 1960s with the rise of the motor car, travelling by rail was on the decline. The station was no longer as busy as it once was, but it retained a direct service to London – and it still had its roof. This had unfortunately gone by the time of the station's 150th anniversary in 1997. (*Ken Carsey*)

Suffolk Terrace, London Road North, *c.* 1980. Liptons new store on the corner of Denmark Road and London Road North opened in December 1974 following the demolition of the Suffolk Hotel. The four shops to the right of the new supermarket were known as Suffolk Terrace, named after the original Suffolk Hotel built in the eighteenth century, and which covered much of the site until its demolition in 1874. In the 1980s, shops here included Irene's bridal fashions (next to the new supermarket), and which had been acquired by Chadds in 1971. Coles the Chemists at no. 41 also had a branch on the corner of Norwich Road. I remember a full-size cutout figure in a swimsuit leaning against the shop front in London Road North promoting Kodak film. The Card Shop at 43 had been Spashett's toy, wool and stationery shop from the 1870s until 1934 when it became the Chain Library. Braham's at no. 45, who had replaced their bay window with a large modern shop front, later became a branch of Palmers. It had been Liptons from the 1920s to 1964. Lloyds Bank's austere front almost defies anyone to enter! The banner across the road promoted a concert and arts and crafts fair at St Margaret's church. The stops for both the town buses and Eastern Counties, and the missing steeple of St John's date the photograph to between 1978 and 1983. On a fashion note: only one man is wearing a pair of flares. (*Ken Carsey*)

Jarrolds, London Road North, 1987. A business from Norwich which came to Lowestoft during the town's expansion in the early years of the last century, it was opened in 1907 initially as a stationers. By the 1980s it was a much loved and popular shop, especially for those looking for local books. Regretfully, its small size was a problem and being unable to expand, it closed in September 1996. (*Author*)

Postwar shops, London Road North, 1980. Barclays moved from the corner of Commercial Road in 1964 into premises designed by Tayler & Green, and built to replace shops damaged in the war. Currys, an old established national bicycle and electrical shop, opened their branch here in December 1964, after demolishing part of the old house that stood on the corner of Surrey Street. (*Ken Carsey*)

Chadds department store, London Road North, 2000. The store extends across what were once three separate buildings, including this imposing premises originally constructed for Flood & Son, printers and stationers, in 1902. It later became the Coronet Cinema until the early 1920s, when it was renamed the Theatre de Luxe.

Chadds was founded in 1907 by George Bertie Chadd. The store as we know it today began in 1913, at nos 70 and 72 London Road North (the site of today's main entrance). Primarily a ladies' and gentlemen's outfitters, by 1926 Chadds had expanded to include nos 68 and 74. After George Bertie's death in 1940, the greatest increase, not only in the size of the store but also its diversity, including a number of branches in Lowestoft and Southwold, took place when his son, George Victor Nudd Chadd, became chairman in 1948 following a distinguished war career. Under Colonel Chadd, as he was popularly known, the store expanded in size and scope, covering the site we see today. It became a focal point in the town centre, especially during the summer months when hundreds of flowers in full bloom decorated the front of the store, as seen here.

George Victor Chadd died in June 1997, aged eighty-nine. A former deputy Lord Lieutenant of Suffolk and friend of ex-prime minister Sir Edward Heath, he had continued to run the store until a few months before his death. In his later years he would occasionally be observed sitting in the corner of the store's restaurant taking his lunch-break. Controlling interest in the store was sold to Palmers of Great Yarmouth in March 2004. (*Author*)

Britten Centre bus station, Gordon Road, September 1989. Eastern Counties mini-buses wait in what were once the grounds of the Regent Alfresco Theatre, opened in 1919. It was bought by Eastern Counties in the 1930s and turned into a bus station. The theatre itself was turned into a garage. It became part of the Britten Centre in 1987. Note the 'Danger' signs. (*Author*)

Eastern Counties' booking office and the entrance to Gordon Road bus station, c. 1981. Until the 1930s, when it was acquired by Eastern Counties, this was the main entrance to the Regent Alfresco Theatre from London Road North. Unlike Timpsons and Woolworths next door, the booking office managed to survive the last war only to be demolished in the 1980s. (*Ken Carsey*)

Jan Kubelik, 1903. This famous young violinist visited Lowestoft in July 1903 performing at the Public Hall in London Road North. Kubelik's reputation was equivalent to today's pop stars; his looks guaranteed his popularity with the ladies, including those in his Lowestoft audience.
This portrait was sent to a Miss Hattie Mitchell at Kessingland, who may have been among them.

Shops on the site of the Public Hall, London Orad North, 1983. The empty premises between Mackays and Dales is the approximate location of the Public Hall. Built in 1873, it was destroyed in February 1941 with other buildings close by. Almost the whole terrace was obliterated. Rebuilding started in the early 1950s with this final block completed in the early 1960s. (*Ken Carsey*)

Morlings, 141–51 London Road North, August 2006. Founded in 1892 by Ernest Morling in Old Nelson Street, like Tuttles and Chadds, Morlings the House of the Music was another well known family business to be found in the town centre. Following his first shop in London Road North – at no. 186 in the early years of the twentieth century – Ernest then moved his music shop to no. 149 in 1906. The business subsequently expanded into no. 151 by 1930. The original shop was destroyed during the war, a period in which the family also suffered; not only were the Morlings bombed out of two shops, nos 149–51 and no. 160 opposite, the third move into 106 London Road North unfortunately coincided with the Waller Raid in January 1942 which decimated much of the town centre. Among those killed on that fateful day was Ernest himself. After moves into the High Street and to 81 London Road North, reconstruction began in 1954. The new premises at nos 149–51 were opened in 1955 by the internationally renowned pianist, Benno Moiseiwitsch.

Morlings was essentially a music shop, selling everything from instruments and sheet music to gramophones and records. From the 1930s, the shop expanded into radios and in later decades into televisions. In more recent years, Morlings also dealt in electrical goods. Their move to London Road South in July 2006 saw a return to their roots – music and musical instruments.

In its long history Morlings has paid host to many great musicians during their stay here and is remembered as the haunt of Lowestoft's claims to musical fame including composer Benjamin Britten and more recent pop idols such as The Darkness and Li'l Chris. (*Author*)

A Lowestoft Corporation bus approaches the Arcade bus stop, London Road North, 1960s. Taken from a bus travelling in the opposite direction, the Victoria Arcade itself had been destroyed in 1941, however the stop kept its old name 'The Arcade' into the 1980s. Taken after the arrival of Tesco's in 1964, the steeple on the horizon belongs to St John's church. (*Author*)

The Arcade bus stop, London Road North, *c*. 1980. Postwar reconstruction began in 1957 with the Co-operative store being one of the first to be built. Aldreds estate agents are still there, however Sudbury Carpets were replaced by Heil's Café in the mid-1980s. In front of Sudbury Carpets, the location of the bus stop gives some idea where the entrance to the Arcade once was. (*Ken Carsey*)

Upper part of London Road North, *c.* 1980, looking towards the High Street and seen in its final days as a through route. To the left is the Trustees Savings Bank, enlarged in about 1981. The route towards the Bridge now travelled down Old Nelson Street and Battery Green Road. The Fox and Hounds, no longer a public house, had become Lawrence Gall's book shop. (*Ken Carsey*)

Lowestoft Co-operative Society Central Stores, Clapham Road, *c.* 1912. Founded in 1890, this was the headquarters of the Co-operative Society in Lowestoft – every product found there was made in factories or workshops connected with the Co-operative movement. Over the years, other branches opened as the town expanded; Kirkley in 1903, Norwich Road in 1905, Oulton Board in 1911. Sussex Road (opened in 1912) and Bridge Road, also in Oulton Broad, concentrated on groceries. A dairy was also established at Walton Road in 1927. The Co-operative Wholesale Society took an even bigger interest in the town when it acquired the Maconochie factory on Waveney Drive in 1929 producing canned herring and tinned vegetables. The most famous brands produced at Lowestoft and which were available in co-operative shop throughout the country, were 'Jenny' canned herrings and 'Waveney' tinned vegetables.

The Lowestoft Central Stores survived until 3 July 1940, when they became a casualty of the first daylight raid on Lowestoft of the Second World War. The building was completely destroyed except for one corner; four people were killed. Following the acquisition of the site by Lowestoft Borough Corporation in 1964, it became one of several proposed locations for a new civic building.

Opposite, bottom: Lowestoft School of Motoring, corner of Clapham Road and Alexandra Road, 1984. The home of the Latter Day Saints from 1913 to about 1929, this corner was all that survived after the Co-operative Central Stores next door received a direct hit in 1940. Lowestoft Corporation bought the premises and the bomb-site next door in 1964. At the time of writing it belongs to Waveney District Council. (*Ken Carsey*)

Bevan Street East, August 2000. Bevan Street, like Clapham Road, is a continuation of the commercial centre that grew around the railway station from the 1850s. Originally known as Chapel Lane, it initially followed an eccentric route to Rotterdam Road, part of which became Norwich Road. It was renamed Bevan Street in the 1870s, and developed into a busy shopping centre in its own right. In 1976, it was cut in half by Katwijk Way, the town's first spinal relief road, turning what became Bevan Street West – now cut off from the town centre – into a residential area. Meanwhile, Bevan Street East continued much as before. The hairdresser is still on the corner of Clapham Road, as is Ann's Café next door, but although only taken eight years ago, even this view has become a bygone sight. As part of the Waveney Sunrise Scheme, Bevan Street East became more pedestrian-friendly. However, already suffering from flooding from heavy downpours and overflowing drains – the most recent being in August 1999 – the roadway, already higher than the pavement, was heightened again. The large block at the end of the road is McDonalds, built in 1974 as Liptons supermarket. (*Author*)

Tudor Lodge, 16 Surrey Street, *c.* 1930. At one time Surrey Street was a continuation of the villas to be found in London Road North, albeit not on such a grand scale. In 1927, Tudor Lodge was the home and surgery of Dudley Boswell, who was also medical officer to the Poor Law Institution. It and the terrace next door were destroyed by bombing in 1941.

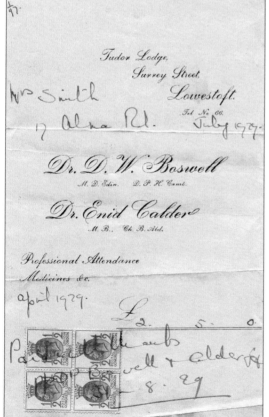

Bill for medical services, Tudor Lodge surgery, July 1929. Two years later and Enid Caulder had joined Dudley Boswell as a partner at Tudor Lodge. After the war, Doctor Calder and John Boswell, Dudley's son, had a surgery in Gordon Road. My own recollection of Doctor Calder was that she bred bulldogs. Occasionally one would sit in her surgery eyeing up four-year-old boys, it seemed to me, for its dinner!

Bridge Terrace, mid-1960s. There had been a terrace of shops in existence here since the 1860s. This branch of Yarmouth Stores had been here since the 1920s, while Thains wet fish shop and restaurant expanded from corner premises into what had been Reliance Photographic Services (on the right). A Lowestoft Borough Corporation AEC Regent makes its way towards the Bridge and Pakefield via London Road South. Route four connected the Gunton Estate in north Lowestoft to Long Road and Elm Tree Road on the periphery with Carlton Colville, which was mainly countryside. In 1964, Corporation bus fares cost 2½d up to half a mile with the most expensive journey in the town costing a whopping 8d. Between the bus and the canvas shade is the Eastern Counties booking office where summer trips to various parts of Norfolk and Suffolk, including Witchingham Wildlife Park and the Queen's estate at Sandringham could be had. Naturally there was also the ever-popular Mystery Tour that every coach operator seemed to organise and which always ended up at some out of the way country pub. The terrace was demolished in 1970 to make way for the temporary road bridge when the Swing Bridge seized up in the open position in 1969. (*Kenny Harper*)

3

South Lowestoft

Kirkley and South Lowestoft from the sea, *c.* 1954. Pile drivers are working on the sea wall, repairing damage caused by flooding in early 1953. On the cliffs are St Luke's Hospital (left), St Mary's Convent and the Victoria Hotel (centre). The winter high tide gives some idea of the threat hampering the cliffs at Pakefield and Kirkley.

St John's Church, London Road South, *c.* 1899. Built in 1853 by Lucas Brothers to designs by John Louth Clemence, the clock was added in 1887 to commemorate Queen Victoria's Golden Jubilee. Between the church and Pier Terrace is a street crossing, surprisingly unattended by a crossing sweeper. Both the floods of 1897 and 1953 caused damage to the church's Caen stone and despite attempts to save it, St John's was demolished in 1977.

On the Esplanade, 15 April 1914. Somewhere in the crowd that particularly warm Easter Wednesday is the anonymous sender of this postcard. The weather brought a lot of people out; however, the National Union of Teachers' conference was being held in the town that week, and the Suffragettes were also in Lowestoft. Reports were rife that Mrs Pankhurst was to speak in the town that day.

Newsagents, 61 London Road South, *c.* 1980. Situated between Ibberson's Central Garage (left) and Wrights motorcycles (right), it had been Cowles confectioners and newsagents from about 1951 into the 1970s. Originally 19 London Road South, from 1869 to 1898 it was one of several photographic studios serving the south Lowestoft resort. It remained a newsagents until the late 1990s. (*Ken Carsey*)

Windsor Road, 25 April 1916. Four soldiers pose for their portraits following the German naval bombardment earlier that day. The squadron attacked the town at four in the morning before being chased off by British naval vessels. The shell that hit these houses in Windsor Road also destroyed the upper floors of Edgar's photographic studio in London Road South. This unusual photograph was one of a series of stereoscopic photographs published by a London company.

London evacuees arriving at the Claremont Pier, 1 September, 1939. Although war was declared on 3 September, plans were already afoot to move the capital's children out of the expected firing line. For some reason Norfolk and Suffolk were considered as safe areas. This group of children came up from Dagenham by the paddle-steamer *Royal Daffodil*. Each child carried a gas mask and a small amount of personal belongings. They arrived complete with a tag tied to their clothing saying who they were. The two men standing on the right of the photograph are Selwyn Humphrey, then deputy mayor, wearing glasses and sporting a beard and moustache, who was among officials who met the children and their school teachers at Lowestoft, and in the foreground, nearest to the camera, is Mr G. Wright (in white shoes). The *Royal Daffodil* with its sister ship *Royal Eagle* eventually evacuated 3,500 children from Essex. After a short rest the children were then moved into the Norfolk countryside. The evacuation also marked the end of regular paddle steamer services.

Stead & Simpson, 219–21 London Road South, 1996. Then Lowestoft Barbecue takeaway, from 1902 to the 1980s it was the Kirkley branch of Stead & Simpson. Speedy Repair Service next door at no. 223 (on the left) had been run as a boot and shoe repair service by Mr Normanton since the late 1940s, while previously Charles Metcalf had his photographic studio here from 1916 to the late 1920s where he could be observed standing at the entrance wearing a grey, once-white, coat and a large hat! (*Author*)

London Road South, *c.* 1984. Looking south from Waterloo Road, Prontoprint is now Kirkley Village Press. Next door, at no. 160, was Vera Porter's restaurant from the 1930s to the 1990s. Vera died in 2000, aged eighty-seven. Although the shops have altered little, the street today is part of Waveney's Sunrise Scheme. Traffic now travels along Tom Crisp Way towards the Bridge. (*Ken Carsey*)

Henry's Emporium, London Road South, 1980. Henry's was one of a number of second-hand shops once to be found throughout Lowestoft. Built in the back garden of a house in Marine Parade, I remember the single-storey shop mainly in its final days when dampness began to make its mark, especially on LP records and their covers. (*Ken Carsey*)

Lilians, London Road South, Kirkley, 1980. Founded as a milliners in 1935, it was taken over by Miss Sparkes as Lilians, and expanded into drapery as well as ladies' and children's outfits. Its success meant it eventually stretched into five shops, 198–206 London Road South. Lilians was acquired by Chadds in 1956. However, it was one of the first to suffer in Kirkley's decline and closed in 1991. (*Ken Carsey*)

Leather-Luxe, London Road South, Kirkley, 1980. Part of Walker-Regis, its main branch was in London Road North. Located next to Lilians (on the right, out of camera), with Matthams, watchmaker and jeweller to the left. (*Ken Carsey*)

Pier Terrace, *c.* 1980. Curtiss Restaurant moved here from 125 London Road North following the acquisition of their north Lowestoft site in 1964 by Tesco, for their first supermarket in the town. Curtiss had taken over the old Waller Restaurant which had been there since 1887. H.E. Warnes' cycle shop at 2 Pier Terrace was originally Henry Bevan's photographic studio. Established in 1874, Henry Jenkins bought the studio from Bevan in 1896. Both Jenkins and his son, Ford, gained a reputation as photographers of many of the port's fishing vessels. The studio moved over the Bridge to 11 London Road North (now 11 Station Square) in 1955. Norfolk Travel Agency, part of Norfolk Motor Services, was at 2a Pier Terrace. The company was based at Great Yarmouth, but occasionally could be found with other coach operators on the Royal Plain, the general collection point for day trips as far afield as Stanway Hall Zoo near Colchester, or to Cromer on the north Norfolk coast – or just for an evening's trip, guaranteed to stop at a 'mystery' roadside inn on the way. Norfolk Motor Services eventually closed in 1985. (*Ken Carsey*)

Demolition of St John's Church, 1978. The remains of the interior of the church as seen from London Road South; two floods (1897 and 1953) and Lowestoft's unforgiving sea air ate into the church's fabric and left St John's in a pitiful state by the early 1970s. St John's steeple disappeared from the skyline in late 1977, and in the early months of 1978 the rest of the church was demolished. St John's School, also built in the 1850s, survived for a while longer. The clock, which had been erected in the jubilee year of one queen (Victoria in 1887) and taken down in the jubilee year of another (Queen Elizabeth II) ninety years later, had reportedly disappeared into the hands of a collector.

St John's had been built in 1853 as the parish church to Sir Morton Peto's New Town resort, which in later years also took in part of an area north of the Bridge including Bevan Street and Denmark Road. A hundred years later, in the floods of 1953, it would also be the scene of a spectacular rescue by two row boats of some thirty people, including six children, stranded in the church and the neighbouring St John's School hall, as the flood waters rose ever higher. (*Ken Carsey*)

St John's School, St John's Road, *c.* 1970. Built by Lucas Brothers in the grounds of St John's Church, it retained to the end many early Victorian features such as its Italianate decoration seen here on the chimneys. After surviving the floods of 1897 and 1953 it ended its days as one of the town's first night shelters.

Royal British Legion hut and Colville Hall, Clifton Road, 1993. Opened in 1899 as St Matthew's Church, and seen here from Beaconsfield Road, Colville Hall is another church no longer with us. Following its closure in 1914, it spent many years as a community centre, before becoming the Open Brethren meeting room in the 1960s. Derelict for some time, it was demolished as recently as 2008. (*Author*)

St John's Church, *c.* 1954. Looking across from the North Quay with Pier Terrace on the left, St John's School is on the corner of St John's Road (to the right of the bow of LT166 *Gypsy Queen*). The southern end of Pier Terrace was demolished in 1964 following subsidence caused by the 1953 floods. The *Gypsy Queen*, a trawler built in Hessle in 1950, became a total loss in January 1955.

Nos 174 to 180 London Road South, Kirkley, 1970s. The photographer Ken Carsey was always on the lookout for unintentional humour such as these three shops in Kirkley. The Carlton Fish Restaurant is on the left, Cooks at no. 178 had been Edgar's photographic studio from 1916 to the early 1960s. Whitings was at no. 180. The photo says it all; Fish Restaurant Cooks (Cook's in this case) Whiting!

Coronet Social Club, London Road South, c. 1978. Very little remained of the old Arcadia Theatre by the time bingo became the rage. Its once-proud frontage had long disappeared by the late 1970s. After some uncertainty as to its fate, the Coronet became the Hollywood in November 1989, and the first of a chain of cinemas stretching across north Suffolk and Norfolk. (*Ken Carsey*)

London Road South, November 1981. Look at those forecourt prices! Two-star petrol at £1.64 a gallon, four-star at £1.66 a gallon. I'm old enough to recall being shocked when petrol reached 50 pence a gallon in the mid-1970s! The filling station disappeared around 2006 to become a KFC drive-in. Looking across to Parade Road South, only Pot Black survives today. (*Ken Carsey*)

Ice Company offices, Riverside Road, 1980. Fred Cockrell had founded the East Anglian Ice Company in 1898; before this, imported Norwegian ice was stored at the thatched ice house on the outer harbour near the swing bridge. In the 1960s this area was one of the sites designated for the proposed third river crossing; however, the building was known to have survived at least to 2006. (*Ken Carsey*)

Lowestoft Corporation bus outside the Grand Cinema, London Road South, 1961. Eastern Coachworks had been building bus bodies at Lowestoft since the factory was set up as an offshoot of the United bus company in 1920. The Grand opened as a cinema the same year. It became a bingo hall in the 1960s. The site is now the Kirkley Centre. Regretfully, the coachworks closed in 1987. (*David Mackley*)

Lake Lothing, late 1890s. The heart of industrial Lowestoft in its Victorian heyday, and looking across from its southern bank towards Oulton Broad, a hundred years earlier as the Freshwater, this would have been an ideal spot for fishing for pike, perch, roach and bream, or to hunt wildfowl. Although a port since 1679, Lowestoft as a harbour was only sixty years old when this photograph was taken on the shores of Samuel Richards' shipyard in Horn Hill, itself only twenty years old. The lake had only been tidal since the 1830s when the lock gates connecting the outer and inner harbours were attacked by the teredo worm, a saltwater mollusc that bored into the wooden hulls of ships, wrecking the lock gates. The lake has been saltwater ever since. As late as the 1890s mudflats could still be seen at low tide. Already Maconochie Brothers had joined Samuel Richards on the south side of the lake, while boat builders, dry docks and warehouses had sprung up from Commercial Road, along the North Quay opposite. The channel on the left was the entrance to Kirkley Ham, which until 1894 separated the Maconochie factory on the western side of the Ham from Richards shipyard on the Kirkley side. In the water, traditional wooden vessels mix with steam, smacks lay side by side with cargo vessels, and the whole north bank as far as Mutford Lock and Oulton Broad is one of industry. The imposing twin-funnelled ship is HMS *Hearty*. On the right are several smacks including one originally from Sunderland. We forget today how wide Lake Lothing once was.

CWS factory and East Anglian Ice Company, Riverside Road, 1934. Seen from the North Quay on the opposite bank with the tugs *Barton* and *Imperial* moored alongside, the factory was built by the two Maconochie Brothers in 1901 and had been acquired by the Co-operative Wholesale Society some years before, in 1929. Richards shipyard would be on the extreme left, just out of camera range.

The CWS canning factory, 1981. Viewed from Richards' shipyard from the top of one of its cranes and looking towards the cranes at Brooke Marine in Heath Road and to Oulton Broad itself, the mudflats have completely disappeared. The waterfront in the foreground marks the entrance to Kirkley Ham, bridged over in 1894 by the Maconochie brothers. Normanston Park is on the opposite bank. (*Ken Carsey*)

Co-op factory and Lowestoft canning factory, Waveney Drive, August 1995. A favourite view with photographers over the decades – myself included – and showing both number 1 and number 2 factories. the latter with its imposing chimney.

The single-storey Lowestoft Canning Factory on the right is an extension of the older of the two buildings, and originally erected in 1891. Taken from the forecourt of the Dial-a-Ride offices in Waveney Drive, now the site of the northern entrance to Tom Crisp Way near the Maconochie roundabout not far from Riverside Road, the larger, more imposing building was built in the early twentieth century and also housed the factory offices. The photographer stands on what was once marshland at the entrance to Kirkley Ham.

Lowestoft Canning closed in October 1994 after employees were given fifteen minutes to clear the building. The remainder of the factory shut in 1997 and demolition started in 1998. With the closure of Richards' shipyard earlier in May 1994, by 2000 and the years immediately following, a once-vibrant part of south Lowestoft became one of the largest open spaces the town has seen since the Second World War. (*Author*)

Launch of the Esja, mid-1980s. The next four pages are dedicated to the vessels and men who worked at Richards' shipyard. Throughout its history Richards' constructed a wide range of vessels, the Esja was built for an Icelandic ferry company. It had no propellers but steered by bow and aft thrusters. There are few trees in Iceland, so she left port full with wooden furniture – and a Mini. (*Ken Carsey*)

Richards' shipyard workers, launch of the *Esja*, mid-1980s. Of those watching the Esja pull away, nearest to the camera and leaning on the gangplank ropes is plater Mike Colby, on the other side of the gangplank is Cyril Potter. Beyond the entrance to Kirkley Ham is the CWS Canning Factory and in the distance, the cranes of Brooke Marine. (*Ken Carsey*)

Outside the engineering shop, Richards', *c.* 1984. From left to right are; ? Donnington, -?-, -?-, Stewart 'Ham-bone' Hammersley and Malcolm Abbott. Young Donnington followed his father and grandfather into the firm. 'Ham-bone' was so-called because he was the workshop's first-aider. (*Ken Carsey*)

HMAFV *Sea Otter*, SLP quay, March 1985. Men from Richards' are preparing HMAFV *Sea Otter* to be converted to HMS *Redpole*. Not all work at Richards' was done at the shipyard itself, however. Other yards or quays were hired as needed, such as the SLP quay. (*Paul Allison*)

Early Richards'-built steam drifter *Resolve* about to pass sailing drifter LT70 *Strive*, 1900. Richards' first steam drifter was the *Test*, launched in 1899; others soon followed. As if to demonstrate the advantages of steam over sail, the *Resolve*, another pioneering Richards' steam drifter, is travelling on an almost dead calm sea, and with three barges in tow is about to pass the sailing smack!

LT100 *Boston Scimitar*, Waveney Herring Dock, 1959. Richards maintained its reputation as a builder of fishing vessels into the 1940s and '50s. The success of a new design of drifter built in the late 1940s for Small & Company, led to a series of diesel trawlers for Boston Deep Sea and to a design which became instantly recognisable as a Lowestoft fishing boat.

LT58 *Boston Pegasus* following its launch at Richards' shipyard, 1954. A diesel trawler built for Boston Deep Sea Fisheries, it was eventually sold in 1971. The vessel is moored alongside Morton's Quay, until 1988 the second of two food factories on the South Quay. The factory chimney was eventually demolished in 1991.

Launch of the *Cromarty Shore*, Richards' shipyard, June 1974. By the 1970s, Richards were also building vessels for the off-shore oil industry. Mrs Mecheline Blinkenhoff (centre with bouquet), wife of the manager of Shell International Exploration and Production, launched the first of two 55m-long oil rig supply vessels built for Offshore Marine Ltd, Great Yarmouth. (*Ernest Graystone*)

Parahaki at Lowestoft, 1963. Moored in the Yacht Basin following sea tests, she was built by Brooke Marine and launched in May 1963. She and her sister ship *Raumanga* were single-screw fire-fighters built for the Whangarei Harbour Board, New Zealand. Both were 130ft long, and each weighed 160 tons. They were fitted with twin 1,500 hp Mirrlees engines giving them a top speed of 12 knots.

Brooke Marine, the second of the two shipyards once to be found on the southern shores of Lake Lothing, was founded in 1874 by John Walter Brooke. Initially, the engineering works were in Alexandra Road, north Lowestoft, where the famous Swan car was built. As Brooke Marine, its main shipbuilding yard was in Heath Road where it built motor boats, cruisers, naval vessels, trawlers and tugs for a variety of customers from across the globe. It was nationalised in 1974 until the mid-1980s when it became Brooke Yachts International. However, the writing was on the wall, and despite building ships such as Richard Branson's much acclaimed *Virgin Atlantic Challenger II*, the yard was finally wound up in 1993.

4

The Resort

Three young ladies stroll along the Esplanade, 1930s. Dressed in the height of seaside
summer fashion and walking towards the Claremont Pier, they were snapped by
L.G. Potter, a local photographer who ran the aptly named Claremont Snaps near by.

The Esplanade and South Beach, *c.* 1897. Sir Morton Peto's new resort was less than fifty years old when this photograph was taken from South Lodge preparatory school. A favourite location for a good view of the sea front and looking north towards the old town, South Lodge was one of many private schools in Lowestoft at the time, and among whose pupils would eventually include Benjamin Britten. Wellington Gardens, on the left, were laid out following the construction of Wellington Terrace in the 1850s. The Esplanade, which was also Lowestoft's first sea wall, was built in the late 1840s as part of Sir Morton Peto's New Town Estate. The cordoned-off stage, centre left on the beach, held regular seaside concert parties for the discerning visitor.

It was said at the time one could tell the success of a resort by the number of bathing machines on its beaches. On the right are just a few of Lowestoft's own bathing machines out that day, tied to capstans just as their forebears had been a hundred years before on the beaches of Lowestoft's first resort at the foot of the cliffs of the old town.

Lowestoft Bridge and the entrance to the resort, *c*. 1899. The first thing the late Victorian visitor and his family to Lowestoft would do after getting off the train at Lowestoft railway station (also built by Sir Morton Peto) would be to make their way by carriage to the town's prestigious New Town resort. It was located across from the north side of the Jubilee Swing Bridge (opened in 1897 to celebrate Queen Victoria's Diamond Jubilee), passing the bridge's control-house (bottom left, this side) and the Harbour cottages on the opposite side. They would either travel towards the Royal Hotel, opened in 1849 and extended a year later, or to Marine Parade and the Harbour Hotel, the only building in the photograph still with us. On the bridge itself – about half way across – making its way towards south Lowestoft, is what is possibly the first motor car in Lowestoft, and appears to be an 1897 Daimler, with a gentleman standing on the rear of the vehicle. It's certainly the earliest photograph I have seen of a motor car in the town.

The Esplanade from Kirkley Cliff, *c*. 1898. The tide may be coming in, but that doesn't stop the bathers. Bathing machines were lined up on the South Beach almost as far as Pakefield. What is missing is the Claremont Pier, built in 1903, and whose entrance would be to the left, just behind the woman with the parasol. The cliff footpath led past the Grand Hotel into Pakefield.

A gentleman visitor and his ward, *c*. 1863. In its early days, visitors staying at the new resort had their portraits taken at James Saunders' studio, not far from Wellington Terrace. The boy wears a new suit for the occasion. His straw hat is tied to the back of his collar, essential on a coast where a bracing summer breeze could make off with one's boater.

The Esplanade and beach, *c.* 1930. Looking past the Claremont Pier with St Luke's Hospital in the distance, the resort attracted photographers such as the Belgian Louis Levy, who had visited Lowestoft before the First World War. The Hatfield Hotel is to the right of the lamppost, the Esplanade Private Hotel is the large modern house with the two large square bay windows, also on the right.

A gentleman and his wife out for a stroll, 1930s. Another photograph taken outside the Claremont Pier by L.G. Potter, one of many photographers plying their trade on the Esplanade between the wars. What is interesting here are the Claremont Snaps' 'your picture here' display boards on the right. Customers would buy copies of their portraits from the Claremont Photo Stores nearby.

Kirkley Cliff, looking north towards Wellington Terrace, 1870s. This was an extension to Peto's resort seen in the distance and was built mainly as boarding houses and private hotels. Here in all its original glory, the road has yet to be laid. The trees in Wellington Terrace mews can be seen between Wellington Terrace and the houses on the Esplanade (right). Cliff Road is on the extreme left.

A sportsman and his bicycle, early 1890s. An all-metal descendent of the penny-farthing, bicycles of all types were ideal modes of transport for journeys around Lowestoft and the surrounding countryside. Parish churches, pretty villages and wayside hostelries on the shores of the River Waveney as far as Somerleyton, St Olaves and Burgh St Peter, made for pleasant rides during the summer months.

South Pier and Pavilion, *c.* 1898. The South Pier Pavilion opened in 1891 following the fire
in 1885, which not only destroyed the original Reading Room but part of the pier itself. The
kiosks at the entrance, dating back to the 1850s and seen here on the left, remained in place
at the entrance to the pier until after the last war. Titan stands on his pedestal through all
the activity around him, wrestling with his cornucopia, much as he does today.

Sail was still king, even for those gentlemen whose craft were moored in the Yacht
Basin. Until the building of the Royal Norfolk and Suffolk Yacht Club opposite, most of
these gentlemen sailors stayed at the Royal Hotel, from whose verandah the photograph
was taken, or nearby at one of the houses on the Esplanade itself. Taken late in the season,
the beach to the right of the pier, known then as now as Children's Corner, has several
youngsters paddling in the sea not far from the breakwater. Young boys sit around in groups
near the top of the steps leading down to the beach, keeping themselves separate from the
rest of the children on the Esplanade. The photograph also shows a first for Lowestoft – not
only did Sir Morton Peto develop the New Town estate into a fine resort and built the Fish
Market – Lowestoft also saw the introduction of the first public toilets in England! They
survived until 2004 and the Waveney Sunrise Scheme refurbishment of the Royal Plain.

185. LOWESTOFT. WAR MEMORIAL.

Royal Norfolk and Suffolk Yacht Club, Royal Plain, 1922. Designed by G. & F. Skipper and opened in 1903, over the years the Yacht Club has acted as host to a variety of famous nautical names including Uffa Fox, Chay Blyth and Sir Francis Chichester. Even royalty have been honoured guests here, particularly the Duke of Edinburgh, who first came to Lowestoft as a young prince in the 1930s.

Lowestoft War Memorial, Royal Plain, c. 1923. Looking towards the Harbour Hotel and Pier Terrace, the memorial was dedicated with great ceremony in 1921, replacing the Reeve monument which was duly relegated to Kensington Gardens, opened in the same year. Every year on the Sunday nearest to 11 November, the memorial is the centre of a remembrance parade, as poignant now as it was in 1918.

North Parade, *c.* 1913. Actually, North Parade is where the photographer is standing, the camera is looking at Gunton Cliff Esplanade. During the season the whole of Lowestoft was a resort, including Gunton, its cliffs and the marram grass-covered Denes. Until his death in 1938, the most notable resident on Gunton Cliff was Howard Hollingsworth of Bourne & Hollingsworth fame.

Warren Cottages, Gunton Denes, *c.* 1890s. Built at the foot of Gunton Cliffs even before Lowestoft first became a health resort in the eighteenth century, its location and the freshwater spring nearby meant it was a popular spot with picnickers into the years leading up to the last war. Famous as part of the Lowestoft China Factory, I suspect that it also saw more than a bit of smuggling in its time!

The North Beach, late 1920s. Lowestoft was one huge pleasure ground during the season. While the South Beach was considered the visitor's beach, the North Beach was considered by Lowestoft folk as 'our' beach. Until the 1950s, it retained a wide stretch of sand, which was aided by the planting of marram grass by previous lords of the manor. On top of the cliffs are the houses on Gunton Cliff.

Demolition of the old Bath House, Hamilton Road, c. 1968. Until the 1960s, vestiges of the old resort in north Lowestoft could still be found including this building, part of the Bath House opened in 1824 and close to what had been the South Beach until the arrival of Sir Morton Peto. Lowestoft's first South Beach was subsequently covered by Battery Green Road and the Fish Market.

The New Recreation Ground, 1920s. The heart of the northern part of the resort, the Denes Oval as it became known, was built in the early 1920s on the old town allotments. Proposed in 1920, the recreational grounds combined tennis and badminton courts with a new Model Yacht Pond and swimming pool near the sea wall. Centre left, behind the lone tree, is the original entrance.

Entrance to the Sparrow's Nest Gardens, 1987. North Lowestoft was always popular with the camping and caravanning fraternity; looking down from the Ravine towards the North Denes caravan park, the High Street was literally a walk away up its famous scores. Regretfully both caravan camp and Denes Oval have been badly neglected in recent years. The entrance to the Nest is on the right. (*Author*)

Sparrow's Nest Gardens Theatre, 1914. The Sparrow's Nest house and grounds were bought by the Borough of Lowestoft in 1897. Designed by the borough surveyor, G.H. Hanby, the theatre was built by Boulton & Paul of Norwich in 1913 at a cost of £1,300. For much of its life the theatre played host to almost every performer of note in the country. Thespian Hayden Coffin performed here, and classical pianist Mark Hambourg made several visits from 1919 onwards. Popular stars such as Leslie Hutchinson, who also returned after the war, and the great bass Paul Robeson, also visited the theatre.

The Sparrow's Nest became HMS *Europa* for the duration of the Second World War. As the headquarters of the Royal Naval Patrol Service, some of its ratings included professional musicians such as saxophonist Freddy Gardiner, who in peacetime had worked for several well-known dance bands. A few also played in the Nest's own dance band, the Blue Mariners, which also recorded as well as made several broadcasts. The BBC had used the Sparrow's Nest Theatre for live broadcasts in the 1930s and continued to do so from 1947 into the 1960s.

Despite a decline in audience numbers in later years, stars of the calibre of Frankie Howerd and Dick Emery made appearances here, but by the late 1980s, and with the choice of the Marina as the town's civic theatre, the building became neglected. Joe Brown and the Bruvvers gave the final show in 1989 and despite calls for it to be saved and renovated, Sparrow's Nest Theatre was demolished in 1991.

Receiving donations, Sparrow's Nest Gardens, 10 July 1937. The Duchess of Kent visited the town in the summer of 1937 to lay the foundation stone for the Nurses' Home in Alexandra Road. During her stay she attended the Hospital Development Fund presentation at the Sparrow's Nest and is seen here on the Nest's open-air stage, seated between the two standing ladies.

Jack Rose and Lisa Mann, Lowestoft War Memorial Museum, Sparrow's Nest, c. 1996. Jack and Lisa are standing beside the lectern presented to the museum. For many years Jack Rose dreamed of a memorial to the men and women who were based, or who lived in the town and who lost their lives during the war. Opened in May 1995, the museum also has its own chapel. (*Mrs Liddy Mann*)

Children's Corner, South Beach, *c.* 1950. Returning south of the bridge, the war-damaged South Pier Pavilion looks on as Lowestoft returns to its peacetime holiday season. Taken from the verandah of the Royal Hotel, postwar reconstruction went hand in hand with surviving remnants of the war. Although the South Pier Pavilion suffered a near miss in December 1940 which destroyed its bandstand and part of the pier, the greatest damage to the building itself was caused while it was in the hands of the Admiralty. It remained in naval hands for some time after the end of the war before being handed back to the town. The building had been so badly neglected that it was demolished in May 1954. The small breakwater of the Children's Corner of the 1890s had now been replaced by a more solid structure, creating a wider beach and a comparatively safer area for younger children to paddle in.

The old South Pier Pavilion was not the only part of the resort to be lost because of the war; both the swimming baths on the North Denes and the ancient Warren Cottages on Gunton Denes had to be demolished. The Royal Hotel, however, once the pride of Sir Morton Peto's superior resort, survived only to be demolished in 1973.

5

The Fishing Industry

Lumpers unloading the catch ready for auction, *c*. 1970. Although conditions were improving by the late 1960s, those working on the fish market still needed to be hardy, especially in the winter months. For some reason the legs of the left-hand lumper appear to be padded with sacking. The boat on the left is LT537 *Suffolk Challenger*, built in 1968 for Small & Co. (*Ernest Graystone*)

Gutting herring, late 1890s. Whether on land or on sea, fishing has always been a hard life. Unlike his fellow contemporaries, this anonymous professional photographer chose not to glamorise the conditions the women on the pickling plots had to endure. Taken on the North Denes next to the Steam Laundry in Whapload Road on what is now part of Birds Eye, this is one of only a few images showing the harsh conditions the women, mainly Scots who followed the fishing down along the East Coast, had to endure during the winter months at Lowestoft. The fog in the background may either be haze from nearby smokehouses or, as the photograph appears to have been taken late in the season (which lasted from September to November), it was more likely to be the result of the bitterly cold weather. And there was no protection on the North Denes from the icy winds blowing in from the North Sea.

Each year every available open space in the town was taken up as a herring processing plot. The Denes were no exception and were given over to the gutting, pickling and packing of the 'silver darlings'. The girls would protect their fingers not only from the sharp knives, but also against the salt and brine, working through the night illuminated by oil lamps. By the end of the season overnight temperatures could occasionally drop to below freezing. Many of the women here are barely out of their teens, some are already married; a few even bought their bairns – their young children – with them.

Lowestoft Harbour, c. 1900. A Yarmouth smack, YH150 Bonito, approaches Lowestoft Harbour. Scottish and Kentish boats have already joined those crammed in the harbour. Only 10 miles apart, for centuries the fishermen of Great Yarmouth and Lowestoft were bitter enemies; however, with the arrival of the East Coast herring fishery, for a handful of weeks each year the rivalry was forgotten.

Pickling Plots, North Denes, c. 1912. Seen here in the early weeks of the season, all signs seem to suggest that the photograph was taken on the only day of the week the girls had off. Gunton Denes is in the distance and the High Street is on the cliff top. At the foot of the cliffs are the fish-houses in Whapload Road. Everything is open to the elements.

The Rose family, *c.* 1914. Like many families in the town, generation followed generation into the fishing industry. The Capps, Ayers, Durrants, Breaches, Catchpoles and Butchers, among others, all made their mark in what was, and which still is, a tough and dangerous life. Even as late as the 1960s, parents warned their offspring (myself included), 'put one foot on that boat and you are of this house'. It did little to curb many to follow their forefathers into fishing on the North Sea. Prominent fishing families proliferated in the town; the six Rose brothers were a typical example. Standing at the back are, from left to right: John, Arco and Bert, while seated are, also from left to right, George, Charles and Harry.

Charles became the father of local historian Jack Rose (1926–2000), who also followed his father and grandfather into fishing out of Lowestoft. According to Jack, the Rose family arrived in Lowestoft in the eighteenth century when Thomas, an émigré, came to work at the old Lowestoft China factory as a decorator.

Jumbo Fiske MBE, 1970. Successful skippers were heroes; highly esteemed by the boat owners, and greatly respected in their communities. Such a man was Ernest 'Jumbo' Fiske, seen here in a rare informal mood. He was nearly 6ft 6in tall and one of the last of the old type of fisherman once so common in ports as far afield as Lowestoft and Aberdeen. (*Ernest Graystone*)

Ex-skipper 'Twee' Utting and his wife Hilda at home in Kessingland, September 1974. His nickname passing down from his father, 'Twee' worked up from cook to skipper spending most of his time on steam drifters. In 1938, as skipper of the *Plumer* he rescued the crew of the drifter *United*. 'Twee' won the Prunier Trophy in 1956 as skipper of the Lowestoft drifter *Silver Crest*. (*Ernest Graystone*)

Off to the herring grounds, *c.* 1920s. If it wasn't the pungent odour of herrings being cured in smokehouses throughout the town, or the haze caused by the smokehouses themselves, it was the vast clouds of smoke being churned out into the atmosphere by the steam drifters making for the fishing grounds. Only a small number of boats here – sailing smacks in the background are raising their sails and waiting their turn, this scene so effectively caught by an anonymous photographer on the South Pier, leaves little to the imagination of the clouds that would be caused by several dozen or even a hundred steam drifters making their way out of the harbour! The steam drifters here include LT1084 *Arimathea* (with its starboard side facing the camera) built in 1907 at Lowestoft; LT572 *Ouse* (light coloured hull, centre right) built in 1900 at Govan and scrapped 1954; LT1060 *Pilot Star* (the steamer on the right) also built in Lowestoft in 1907 and owned by the Star Drift Fishing Company.

In the background almost hidden by the smoke but picked out by the sun, is the shape of Columbus Buildings in Waveney Road, the Lowestoft headquarters of Consolidated Fisheries from 1926 to 1955.

Gutting herrings, *c.* 1907. As the majority of those working here were young women, there was always the chance for the men to have a bit of romance; the couple on the extreme left certainly show signs of a budding relationship, for example. Located on the North Denes, not far from the Sparrow's Nest Gardens, the barrels appear to be so arranged to offer the packers some protection from the weather.

Curing Yards, Hamilton Road, late 1930s. In the distance is Battery Green Road, looking towards the houses in the Marina. The old sailing drifters had all but disappeared; but the work remained just as arduous and still in the open. A postcard sent in May 1941, the writer mentions the film *Harvest of the Sea* and ends with an understatement; 'This is a skilled job'.

Drying Area, North Denes, Whapload Road, *c.* 1920. Drift nets drying on the North Denes were once a common sight particularly during the herring season. The Denes drying area dates back to the time when Lowestoft's fishing boats were moored up onto the beach in front of the cliffs; in the background are the gardens of the houses in the High Street stretching down to the foot of the cliffs. Several of the fish-houses seen here were once owned by the High Street merchants living on the cliff top. Some of these fish-houses were built as early as the seventeenth century, most, however, were constructed in the nineteenth century. At the time of the photograph E.T. Capps and fellow boat-owners Ernie Butcher could be found nearby, mainly on the cliff side. Ayers also had their tannery here.

The drift nets disappeared in the 1960s, following the decline of the herring fishery. Fortunately, some of the old frames remain in place to this day as a reminder of the town's once great fishing heritage.

The nets the men are handling might have been made locally, possibly on the Beach village – the community that arose at the foot of the cliffs – or by net-makers elsewhere in the town such as James Jack & Sons, a Stonehaven net manufacturer with a branch at Lowestoft, or Stuart & Jacks in Clapham Road.

Jones' fish house, Gas Works Road, c. 1960. Terry Jones stands inside one of the smaller fish houses in the old Beach village. They had been T. Jones & Son's premises in the 1920s, and survived as late as 1968 and the building of the town's first industrial estate. Terry was also a relative of Charles Henry Jones who had a smokehouse and wet fish shop in St Peter's Street.

LT651 Acme, 1920s. Travelling towards the harbour mouth with the Trawl Market, Waveney Road and Battery Green Road in the background. Acme is joined by fellow smacks coming out of the Trawl Basin to join her on her way to the fishing grounds. Sail remained popular with smaller boat owners in Lowestoft especially in the early 1920s.

LT80 *Granby Queen, c.* 1956. A diesel trawler built in Aberdeen in 1954 for Talisman Trawlers, she was based in Lowestoft until 1967 when she was sold to the Hazael Fish Company and renamed the *Brenda Wilson.* Younger members of the crew stand at her bow as she makes for the fishing grounds. With the introduction of new technology it was no longer a case of relying purely on instinct in detecting fish stocks, these young crewmen had now to get to grips with sonar in hunting down the catch. The Lowestoft headquarters of Boston Deep Sea Fisheries, who took over Consolidated's building in 1955, can be seen in the background.

Towering over the *Granby Queen*'s wheelhouse is the four-storey building on the corner of Suffolk Road and Waveney Road, once the headquarters of Samuel Richards who not only built fishing vessels, but at one time in the early decades of the twentieth century also ran his own fleet. This tall, red-bricked building constructed in 1890 also housed some of the businesses owned by other members of the Richards family including his photographer son, Lewis, who later became a director of the shipyard following his father's death in 1919. By the late 1950s it housed the offices of fish merchants J.T. Cole as well as solicitors Lovewell Blake. The large roof flanked on either side by two square towers is the Hippodrome, built in 1905. At one time a music hall and later a cinema, from the 1960s it was a bingo hall until its destruction by fire in 1999. In its heyday before the First World War, stars such as Florrie Forde, Lottie Collins and the Fred Karno troupe complete with a young and relatively unknown Charlie Chaplin, appeared here. (*Ernest Graystone*)

A406 *George Robb*, *c.* 1959. Scots boats had been a familiar sight at Lowestoft since the nineteenth century and the town's first purpose-built fish market. Taken by an unknown photographer just after her refit, she was named after George Robb of George Robb & Sons, Aberdeen. Built in 1930 as a steam trawler, she was converted at Lowestoft in 1959, regretfully she sank a year later.

LT179 *Gula* coming into the outer harbour, 1950s. Built by Richards in 1936, she and her sister ship *Rewga* are believed to have been two of Lowestoft's 'small ships' that took part in the evacuation at Dunkirk in 1940. After the war, the Gula became part of the Colne fleet until 1972. It was sold for scrap in 1986.

Rossfish office and factory, Trawl Market, taken a few weeks after its closure in early 1982. In its day Ross was the largest employer on the Fish Market with well over a hundred men and women. In the background is part of the up-and-coming SLP oil and gas rig site in Hamilton Road. The closure of the Ross factory in February 1982 was the first sign that all was not well in Lowestoft's fishing industry. (*Author*)

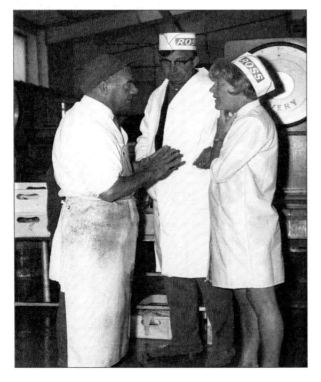

Comedienne Dora Bryan and her husband (centre) with packing foreman Ted Saunders, Rossfish factory, Trawl Market, *c.* 1970. A rare view of the interior of the factory, Dora was at summer season at Great Yarmouth at the time. Also with her on her visit were her son and daughter. (*Ernest Graystone*)

Ken Coleman, manager of Rossfish, October 1975. Taken on the Trawl Dock, with the offices of Small & Co. and Colne Shipping in Waveney Road in the background, this portrait goes to show that even the best photographers can have a bad day. Ken is neither growing an antenna out of his head nor has he something sticking out of his ear! They belong to one of the Boston boats moored behind him. However, this is the only portrait I have of Ken on the Fish Market itself and the only one I have showing him with the Ross factory (in the background on the right).

Despite the loss of the herring, Lowestoft's fishing industry in fact continued to expand. Ross was based in Grimsby, and had only a small branch on the market. Taking over Explorator in 1965, within five years Ross had built a new fish processing plant on the old Trawl Market. Its first manager was the charismatic Gerry Raines, who took over the reins from Explorator's retiring managing director, Stanley Stevens, who continued as a director with Small & Co. In the short time Gerry was at Lowestoft he did much to establish the new fish processing factory. He eventually moved to Hull in 1968, after handing over the reins to Ken Coleman. Ken continued to run the factory until the dark days of the early 1980s, when as the largest company on the Fish Market, Ross was also the first to suffer in the collapse of the industry at Lowestoft.

Whereas Gerry Raines ran the fledgling company as a tight ship, I recall Ken's regime as a bit more relaxed, probably because of the small size of the office block. With both men and women employed in the office, I draw a veil over some of our Christmas parties! (*Ernest Graystone*)

LT419 *Jamesina* about to tie up next to the old Herring and Mackerel Market, *c.* 1980. In the late 1970s a new breed of fishing boat made its appearance at Lowestoft – the beam trawler. For two decades following the demise of the herring, Lowestoft became a major plaice and cod port. With the emphasis on trawling, this boom was not to last. Problems arose as early as 1973 when Lowestoft and Belgian boats were among those reported using large chain mats to trawl up the sea bed disturbing the fish stock's breeding and feeding grounds. Over-fishing and the inherent problems of trawling the bottom of such a shallow body of water as the North Sea saw later decades continue their concerns over the depletion of fish stocks.

The Fish Market was rebuilt in 1987, but any improvements came too late. The Trawl Market, complete with the Rossfish factory, was demolished in the 1990s. The modern fish market fits in quite snugly on part of the old Herring Market seen here; its size today is reminiscent of the first purpose-built market constructed in the 1850s by Sir Morton Peto. (*Author*)

Trawl Basin, 1963. Taken on a dull day with only a handful of weeks before the start of the port's penultimate herring season; moored alongside the quay is LT246 *Fellowship* built in 1931 at Goole as a steam drifter. Among those in the background is LT326 *Yellowtail* constructed in 1945 and rebuilt in Lowestoft in 1959. She had an ignominious end as a derelict houseboat moored near Mutford Lock.

The Fish Market and Harbour, 1964. Taken from the South Pier tower, within three years this drifter would be converted to trawling with plaice superseding herring as Lowestoft's main catch. Looking towards Ness Point, which is hidden behind the gasworks, the boat is about to go into the Inner Harbour.

Selling the first kit of fish from the *Suffolk Chieftain*, July 1969. The auctioning of the first kit of fish – plaice, in this case – from a new boat's maiden trip was always one treated with great ceremony. The *Suffolk Chieftain* was one of a series of diesel trawlers built for Small & Co. and launched at the Appledore shipyard in 1968. Although they were not built in Lowestoft, they were based on designs created for Small by Richards', and which, understandably, Richards' were not very pleased about. *Suffolk Chieftain* arrived at Lowestoft on 24 June 1968 and left for its first trip four days later. It is to my great embarrassment that, despite spending nineteen of my formative years in the fishing industry at Lowestoft, the only one whose name I remember here is Eddie Willis, on the extreme right, who was the fish buyer for Ross. (*Ernest Graystone*)

6

The People

The Ayers family, 1917. Taken at the rear of their butcher's shop at 104 High Street,
I believed James Foster Ayers ran his shop from about 1920 until the late 1950s,
however this portrait suggests he started much earlier. Nevertheless, he maintained a
tradition going back to the 1860s. I hope that those hutches contained nothing more
than the girls' pet rabbits.

The Bird family, 1910. Until the arrival of the cinema and the advent of radio and television, amateur music-making was a popular pastime. Families joined together to form small bands of singers or musicians, as for example, this sextet which included C.F. Bird, Alec Bird, Charles Bird and Claude Bird. Regretfully the names on the back of the print appear not to be listed in any particular order.

Anonymous flautist, Kirkley, *c.* 1863. A portrait taken by pioneer photographer James Saunders, this well-dressed professional musician may also have been a composer, the sheet music in his hand seems to suggest manuscript rather than printed music. It is possible he may have performed at the Town Hall, as well as at the Pavilion Reading Rooms on the South Pier.

Rose Marie, April 1932. A popular operetta by Romberg first performed in London in 1925, the Lowestoft Amateur Operatic and Dramatic Society's own production was very successful in its week-long run at the Marina Theatre. The highlight of the evening was the 'Totem Pole Dance' led by the star of the show, Gladys Munford, who played Wanda the Indian Squaw.

Mabel, Lowestoft Gilbert & Sullivan Opera Club's production of *The Mikado*, 1925. Savoy operas have always had a special place in the hearts of audiences in Lowestoft. The club was founded by Captain Jenkyn and its production at the Marina Theatre that March was held to raise money for Lowestoft Hospital and the Lowestoft Maternity and District Nursing Association.

The cast of *Miss Hook of Holland*, Marina Theatre, February 1922. Lowestoft Amateur Operatic and Dramatic Society's production that year appeared not to be one of their best performances, according to the *Lowestoft Journal*'s reporter on the first night. Held in aid of Lowestoft Hospital and Nursing Association, it may have been first night nerves but the leading lady, Evelyn Gray, who played Sally, the 'Miss Hook of Holland' of the title, although gifted with 'a sweet voice', took a little time to find herself. The conductor, A.E. Mallett, also had some problems with the orchestra and according to the same reporter, had to 'smarten up' his band of players. The photograph was taken on the stage of the Marina Theatre by Christopher Wilson, whose studio was on the corner of the Prairie, not far away in London Road North.

HMS *Hearty* at Lowestoft, *c.* 1898. Granted, this is an unusual place for a photograph of a ship; however, HMS *Hearty* has a close connection with the Lowestoft Amateur Operatic and Dramatic Society. The ship had been the local fisheries protection vessel which tended to visit the town more on pleasure bent than on official business. One of its officers was a Lieutenant W.H. D'Oyly, a relation of Rupert D'Oyly Carte of the D'Oyly Carte Opera Company and Gilbert and Sullivan fame. With a fair amount of talent already on board the vessel, Lieutenant D'Oyly decided to form a concert party. Their performances met with great success, raising money for a number of charities, including a cot for Lowestoft Hospital.

The initial concert party ended when HMS *Hearty* was replaced in 1901 by HMS *Halcyon*, but the popularity of Lieutenant D'Oyly's shows led directly to the formation of an amateur society under the auspices of R.C. Luxon – the Lowestoft Amateur Operatic Society. Needless to say, one of the earliest productions of the new society included *The Gondoliers*. Gilbert and Sullivan operas remained popular throughout the society's existence, but this did not stop the society from staging more recent productions such as *Miss Hook of Holland* and Edward German's *Tom Jones.*

The Revd Evan C. Morgan, rector of St Margaret's, 1920s. Photographed at St Margaret's rectory in the High Street, he was ordained in 1896, and inaugurated as rector of Lowestoft in March 1917. He left Lowestoft in 1931 for the Isle of Wight. Despite his Welsh name, he came from a family of Norwich brewers. He was also the last incumbent to live in the old rectory.

Canon Hawtrey James Enraught, 1931. Canon Enraught came to Lowestoft in 1931 following the resignation of Evan Morgan. He was interested in the history of St Margaret's, gathering notes for an account of the church and its architectural features. Suffering from ill health for some time, he died in 1938 with his work unfinished. However, he influenced a future Lowestoft historian, Hugh D.W. Lees.

The Revd Albert Tupper-Carey and curates, January or February 1906. The time of year also gives a clue regarding the poor lighting conditions for this portrait. Albert Tupper-Carey (front row, second from the right) was the rector of St Margaret's from 1901 to 1910. Of all the rectors in the last hundred years at St Margaret's, Tupper-Carey remains one of the best remembered. He appears to have been the most photographed, which also gives some idea of his popularity during his time at Lowestoft. An unusual time of year for a group photograph, the weather in Lowestoft in the depths of winter can be extremely inhospitable and the fact that it was taken in the gardens of the Old Rectory in the High Street, built in 1870, which also faced the North Sea, a stiff icy breeze cannot have made for a pleasant sitting!

The message on the back of the photograph, a postcard by Henry Jenkins, was written by a member of the Johnson family of Attleborough, Norfolk, who were also photographers. The Revd Tupper-Carey's later career included missionary canon to the Archbishop of York, eventually ending at Monte Carlo, where he was one of the last to be evacuated just as the Germans were closing in. The rectory itself suffered during the Fokker-Wulf raid in May 1943 which also saw the destruction of the Jubilee Stores opposite on the corner of Camden Street and the High Street.

Opening of the Lowestoft War Memorial Museum, 7 May 1995. The dream of local historian Jack Rose, the museum, complete with its own chapel, commemorates civilians and servicemen and women killed during the last war. Left to right: Jane Jarvis, -?-, Revd Phillip Meader, -?-, Jack Rose, Cllr Stella Bostock, town crier David Bullock. Regretfully, Jack died from cancer in 2000. (*Author*)

Police constable and children, Claremont Road, *c.* 1930. 'Taken on the day we met at Lowestoft', the off-duty policeman on the right may have been stationed at Olive Cottages, Carlton Colville; in 1927 William Barber was the constable in charge there. Ashurst House, run by Mr and Mrs Potter, is in the background. The two donkeys were probably owned by Freddy 'Donkey' Jones.

Inspector 'Nobby' Clarke, *c.* 1960. Inspector Clarke poses next to the southward-bound Arcade bus stop opposite the old Eastern Daily Press and Lowestoft Journal office, the truncated Walkers Stores and the northbound Arcade bus stop. The two police cars are a Humber and a Morris Oxford. Lowestoft police station itself was just round the corner in Regent Road. (*Ernest Graystone*)

PC Lockwood on duty, Lowestoft Carnival, August 1981. A popular character, especially with the motorcycle fraternity, more than one youngster can recall words of wisdom after being stopped by PC Lockwood who is seen here at the Lowestoft Carnival, passing Parade Road South and heading toward the Bridge and the town centre. (*Ken Carsey*)

Group 6, Church Road Infants School, *c.* 1906. The school was opened in 1896 and had approximately 261 infants on its register. Both infants and junior schools were built to educate the children living in the new St Margaret's Estate laid out between the late 1880s and 1913. In 1904 the Infants headmistress was Miss Kate Robinson. The main entrance was in Ipswich Road.

Class 7, Church Road Junior School, 1931. Mr Fordham, the headmaster, is on the left, with form teacher Miss Wood on the right. Most of the pupils are wearing ties, however it appears some have only put them on just for the photographer. The school was renamed St Margaret's Junior School in 1950. The junior block was demolished in 1988, though fortunately the infants' section still survives.

Staff members, Lowestoft College, 1908. Until the years leading to the Second World War, Lowestoft had a number of private schools for the sons and daughters of gentlefolk on both sides of the Bridge. This one was on North Parade overlooking the Belle Vue Park. Taken in the college grounds, left to right are; C.V. Southam, C.H. Widdows, H.P.W. Makin and G.R. Keef.

Form V, Lowestoft College, 1909. Form master H.P.W. Markin is seated in the centre. Compare these boys with those on the previous page. These privileged youngsters' lives were secure, assuming they survived the horrors of the First World War, that is. Writing to Miss H.B. Markin in Cheshire, H.P.W. seemed to be more interested in his knee. How he damaged it, he does not say.

Election postcard from Sir Edward Beauchamp, following his parliamentary success, 1906. Sir Edward won with a majority of 1605 over his opponent Colonel Francis Lucas. Sent in February 1906 to Mr L. Collier of Decoy Farm, Blundeston, the postcard thanked friends and colleagues for a successful campaign. Sir Edward eventually retired in 1922.

Parliamentary elections, Harris Avenue, 17 April 1997. Over ninety years later, a crew from BBC East has acquired the technique of walking backwards! Facing us are, from left to right: Cllr Trevor Carter (partly hidden); Bob Blizzard, then leader of Waveney District Council and parliamentary candidate, and county councillor Nye Owen whose pet dog was mascot for the day. (*Author*)

The arrival of the Prime Minister at Lowestoft, 27 October 1928. Stanley Baldwin is seen at the bottom right, wearing a lone bowler hat among a sea of straw hats, flat caps and ladies' bonnets and in front of the police constable looking right towards his smiling colleague on the extreme right. Photographed as the Prime Minister left Lowestoft Central railway station accompanied by Lowestoft's MP, Gervais Rentoul, seen here in the foreground wearing a trilby and holding a folded newspaper, they then travelled by car to the Conservative Party Conference in Great Yarmouth. They drove through the town with their wives after leaving the railway station amid cheers from the crowd, stated the *Lowestoft Journal* of the time. Gervais Rentoul, had succeeded Sir Edward Beauchamp in 1922, and represented Lowestoft from 1922 to 1934. He was the founder of the Conservative Party's 1922 Committee, and was knighted in 1929. Top centre, to the right of the car and almost hidden by people, is a Lowestoft Corporation tram on the line leading from the Rotterdam Road sheds to Denmark Road and the town centre.

Bill Solomon, Lowestoft Maritime Museum, May 1974. One of the founders of the Lowestoft and East Suffolk Maritime Museum, Bill is holding a shoe kettle, an implement specially designed and used by crews in the days of steam drifters to brew hot water for tea. The shape allowed the kettle to be placed in the entrance of the ship's boiler. (*Ernest Graystone*)

Members of the last Bench of the Lothingland and Mutford magistrates prior to reorganisation, March 1974. Taken outside Lowestoft Police Courts, front row left to right are: J.N. Martin (clerk to the justices), S. Perks, Margaret Chadd, Mrs M. Taylor, Mrs S. Bostock, J.G. Oldham, N. Finch (deputy clerk). Back row, left to right: Capt. R.J. Gooch, J.N. Johnson (chair), B. Blowers. (*Ernest Graystone*)

Mrs Hallam and Roger, *c.* 1914. The wife of Walter William Hallam, solicitor and commissioner of oaths. William had been in ill health for some time before he died aged fifty-two in early October 1915, leaving a widow and young son. This portrait is one of a number collected by a Miss Reenan who was employed by the Hallams as a maid. Regretfully, very few portraits survive of W.W. Hallam himself.

Sidney Thrower, aged approximately fourteen, *c.* 1913. Young Sidney was one of six members of the 1st Carlton (St Mark's) Sea Scouts who lost their lives when their craft sank on the River Waveney in June 1914. Augustus Young, among other local photographers, published postcards of the tragedy, one of the rarest probably being this portrait reproduced from a rival photographer, Stickybacks.

Visit of Lord Jellicoe, 8 July 1925. The Lord Kitchener Memorial Home, located on Kirkley Cliff and overlooking the sea, was officially opened in 1919 for soldiers and sailors who were injured in the First World War. Lord Jellicoe visited the Home in 1925 and to celebrate his visit, local notables led by the mayor and deputy mayor gathered on the gardens on the Esplanade in front of an anonymous photographer's lens to mark the auspicious event. Front row, seated from left to right: Sir Harry Foster, MP for north Suffolk (which included Lowestoft) from 1892 to 1900 and in 1910; W. Barnard, mayor of Lowestoft 1923–5; Lord Jellicoe; Sir Saville Crossley, Lord Somerleyton, a member of the Crossley family from Halifax, manufacturers of Crossley carpets; Ashton Strong [sic] (could this be Ashton Stray, the town clerk?). Back row standing, from left to right: Alfred Jenner, deputy mayor (mayor in 1922–3), W.R. Robinson, manager of Ford's shoe shop in London Road South, and head of the town's advertising committee. He was also a photographer and is believed to have hailed from Lincolnshire; Lieutenant Commander Elson, HMS *Liffey*; Sir John Field Beuk; Brigadier General Sir Thomas Jackson; A.J. Turner; the Revd F.W. Emms; M.A. Cross, who had a china shop opposite the General Post Office in London Road North.

Lowestoft Naval League Sea Cadet Corps, *c.* 1940. The photograph was taken at the Denes Oval, next to the Sparrow's Nest, the headquarters of HMS *Europa* and the Royal Naval Patrol Service. The corps was formed in 1939 at Roman Hill School. The officers seated in the front row included Petty Officer Gibbons; non-commissioned officer Kenny Hutson; and Captain Tyrell, harbour master.

Evacuation buses, Church Road Senior Girls School, 2 June 1940. Lowestoft was a front line town with an extensive naval base, shipbuilding and munitions factories. After the evacuation of Dunkirk, as the nearest centre of population to enemy territory, it was the turn of Lowestoft's own children to move to safety. Seen from the top of Winnipeg Road, the youngsters were evacuated to Shirebrook, Derbyshire.

Basket makers, W.S. Thain, Clapham Road, Lowestoft, 1906. A record of the start of the osier season of 1906, osier (willow with long stems for use in basket making) has been a little documented, but nevertheless, vital industry in Lowestoft for centuries. Basket production included wares – not just for butchers, bakers, local errand-boys and housewives – but importantly, baskets of all sizes needed for the fishing industry. Starting in a small way as a basket maker in the High Street in the 1870s, Thain's had had their basket, sieve and swill making premises in Clapham Road since the early 1890s. Willow and reeds came locally or from Norfolk, and at one time they could also be found growing along the shores of Lake Lothing and Oulton Broad. Other customers for baskets were the farms and, so it appears, the local clergy, or at least according to the back of this photographic postcard sent in late November 1906 to the Revd B.G.B. Smith at Carlton Colville, when he was requested to send in his order for turnip skeps for the forthcoming season. Traditional style wicker baskets could still be found in use on the Fish Market as late as the 1990s.

7

The Villages

Oulton Broad North station, 1960s. Taken from the corner of Commodore Road, the
signal-box on the left has a mirror used by the signalman to observe the approaching
traffic in Commodore Road. The gates across Bridge Road were manually operated until
the 1970s. The footbridge was demolished in December 1974.

Yacht Station, Oulton Broad, early 1920s. Looking across to the Oulton side of the Broad and Swonnell's Maltings, in the foreground are yachts and cruisers owned and run by Jack Robinson and his family. Apart from the two boats in the foreground, the only other vessel not powered by sails is a small boat on the right used by fishermen. Jack is standing on the left, close to the water and the only one wearing a seaman's cap. Four members of the family are in the motor boat nearest to the camera. Jack was a yacht agent in the years between the wars to his death in 1939. He was a pioneer in opening up the Norfolk Broads to those other than gentlemen fishermen and Norfolk wherries.

The Yacht Station is seen here before the opening of Nicholas Everitt Park; the banks of the Broad were as yet to be made up. The grounds on the left belonged to Broad House, the residence of Henry Reeve Everitt, also known as Nicholas Everitt, from 1910. Following his death in the late 1920s, the house and its grounds were bought by Howard Hollingsworth, who gave them to the town in 1928 as a public park.

The village of Oulton Broad grew out of the development of Mutford Bridge as part of the Norwich and Lowestoft Navigation which allowed wherries and larger cargo vessels to travel between the port of Lowestoft and the city of Norwich. However it was the arrival of the railway in 1847 that really opened up the Broads. It is also worth noting that Oulton Broad is the only Norfolk Broad in Suffolk.

Oulton Broad, 1963. Taken from approximately the same position forty years later, by this time holiday cruisers took the place of those grand old wherry yachts. Swonnell's maltings is in the background. A relative newcomer, W.B. Hoseason, at 89 Bridge Road not far from the Wherry Hotel, was about to make inroads into the Broads holiday industry.

Oulton Broad, 1963. Hand in hand with its postwar popularity went the rebuilding, or in this case the conclusion of the Mutford Lock bridge opened in 1939, and from where the photograph was taken. A Ford Anglia stands on the road which once led to the earlier bridge built in 1894 and which is seen here with weeds growing on either side. The old road remained as a footpath as late as the 1980s.

Oulton Broad floods, 1993. This and the next three photographs show the floods of 21 February 1993; looking from Bridge Road towards the entrance to Nicholas Everitt Park, only the bows of the cruisers and the small motor boats under wraps indicate where the footpath ended and the Broad began. (*Ken Carsey*)

The houseboat *Doris* built by J.W. Brookes in 1931 for Edward Evans, demonstrates how high the tide was at one time that day. With a television aerial fixed to the side nearest the camera, the *Doris*, which once played host to many a celebrity including the Duke of Windsor, had obviously seen better days. (*Author*)

D.O. Jones' electric milk floats were left stranded in the grounds of the Ivy Farm Dairy in Bridge Road. Nearby, two cars dry out after being pushed out of the Lady of the Lake's car park (foreground, under water). (*Author*)

The Lady of the Lake itself was particularly badly hit. The cellars were completely under water and anyone who left their car at the rear of the pub awoke to find it half submerged. The Wherry Hotel on the opposite bank of the Broad narrowly escaped flooding. (*Author*)

Mutford Lock bridge, Oulton Broad, 1991. The prewar bridge was nearing its end. Although completed in 1939, by the 1970s it was clear that Oulton Broad needed a wider bridge to take the increase in traffic, not only of visitors but the number of vehicles travelling between Lowestoft and Norwich each day. Hoseason's is the modern three-storey building, centre left, in Bridge Road. (*Author*)

Mutford Lock Bridge, Oulton Broad, 1991. The crane on the right indicates that work had already started on the new bridge and bypass. The prewar bridge, which was built to the east of the Victorian structure, retained its original lamps to the last. To the right is what, in the 1950s and into the 1970s, was Waller's restaurant. The present bridge was opened in 1992. (*Author*)

Bridge Road, Oulton Broad, *c.* 1900. Looking across from the Carlton Colville side of the Broad, the Wherry Hotel is in the distance. Signs of the old country road with its trees and hedges can be seen on the left, mixing with the development of the village. Behind the children on the right is the Waveney Hotel. And not a car in sight!

Bridge Road, *c.* 1992. Looking in the opposite direction to where the photographer stood ninety years before. Everything has changed, the motor car had taken over the once-quiet lane as Bridge Road became the main route linking north Lowestoft to the city of Norwich and the Midlands. Traffic queues such as this one not far from Victoria Road junction became an everyday hazard.

London Road, Kessingland, *c.* 1905. Originally London Road was part of the Yarmouth to London toll road opened in the 1780s, The new road in effect created a second Kessingland community to that next to the beach. It was at an inn in London Road that a group of eminent local gentlemen including Robert Sparrow and Lord Rous formed what would become the Suffolk Humane Society in 1806.

Kessingland cliffs and beach, early 1920s. In the nineteenth century parts of the old village had already been lost to the sea. Now its once-extensive beach was reduced in size. In the early years of the decade fishing boats moored up on what little was left. Even this was to disappear until in the storm of January 1937, the houses on the cliff top fell to the mercy of the sea.

Henry Rider Haggard, novelist, 1887. Photographed the same year he published *She*, Haggard was born in Norfolk and educated at Ipswich Grammar School. The author of *King Solomon's Mines* travelled to South Africa before returning to England and marrying Louisa Margitson in 1880. He had a summer retreat at Kessingland Grange from 1899 until the 1920s, where his guests included fellow writers Rudyard Kipling and H.G. Wells.

Somerleyton Hall, 1860s. Apart from the Winter Gardens on the left which had been added by Sir Morton Peto in 1856, it is surprising to find that externally Somerleyton Hall remains much the same today as it did when Michael Barrett photographed the hall in the mid-1860s. Taken in the months after Sir Francis Crossley bought the hall following Sir Morton Peto's bankruptcy, it was here in March 1844 that Peto unveiled his plans for a new resort south of the old town of Lowestoft, the arrival of the railway, and a promise to the Lowestoft men that fish landed in the morning would reach the Midland markets the same day. As well as the Hall, Peto created a new model village of Somerleyton situated round a stylised village green. The Victorian Somerleyton Hall was constructed around an earlier Queen Anne house to designs by John Thomas. The photograph is one of only a few known examples which include Barrett's first wife, the figure seated on the lawn engrossed in her book, and who died in the 1870s.

Pupils from Somerleyton School celebrating Warship Week, October 1941. This group was taken by Ernest Graystone, a serving police officer in the village for the duration of the war. Somerleyton School is the thatched building in the background. As the village was a restricted area, particularly around Fritton Lake and Herringfleet, photography was officially prohibited.

Gunton St Peter's church, c. 1940. This is another theoretically 'illicit' photograph, this time taken not by a police officer, but by a schoolboy, regretfully known only as 'Peter', armed with a small, cheap camera, and who lived nearby. To the left is Gunton Old Hall, complete with windows taped up to avoid glass splinters caused by bomb blast.

Pakefield Church, 1920s. Then some distance from the cliff edge, Pakefield church is, in fact, two churches in one, St Margaret's and All Saints'. The building was destroyed in April 1941, when incendiaries were dropped on its thatched roof setting the church ablaze. Until 1934 this part of Pakefield was a separate parish outside the borough of Lowestoft.

Pakefield Street, before 1914. Of the buildings on the left-hand side of the street, the Borough of Lowestoft side, only the Jolly Sailors public house (to the left of the lamppost) survived the ravages of the sea. The ancient cottages were already falling victims to cliff erosion; the Ship Inn, on the right with the landlady dressed in white at the door, would soon follow.

Gunton Church, Lowestoft

Gunton St Peter's Church, 1890s. Although not mentioned, a church was in existence at St Peter's prior to the Domesday survey of 1086. Gunton St Peter was neither a village nor a hamlet, but a manor. One of the best known lords of the manor of Gunton was Hewlin Luson who, according to Edmund Gillingwater writing in 1790, is reported to have discovered 'some fine clay' on his estate in 1756 which led to the foundation of the Lowestoft China Factory. Gunton, like much of north Lowestoft, is on a grey clay. Bricks and pottery were produced at Gunton before 1700 and the last brick-making kiln remained in production to the end of the nineteenth century. The remnants of several clay pits can be found throughout the old manor; some are now ponds, others have been filled in over the years.

Gunton St Peter was restored and enlarged in 1700 by Charles Boyce. Under all that ivy is a round tower, one of several in this part of north Suffolk. To be truthful, it is not strictly a round tower, but oval-shaped. The church underwent renovation in 1988 and the tower, which seemed to have been slightly truncated some time in its history, restored and heightened.

Beyond St Peter's churchyard, to the left of the ivy-clad tower and the south porch, is Gunton St Peter's rectory; to the left of this is one of the outbuildings belonging to Gunton Old Hall, then the home of the Fowlers. Both the house and the rectory were demolished by the early 1960s. The site of Gunton Old Hall is now covered by Gunton Primary School playing field. (*Ann Hubbard*)

ACKNOWLEDGEMENTS

I am indebted to many people who, over the years, have passed on information or who shared personal memories or photographs, in particular to John Robinson for information about the Robinson family of Oulton Broad, Paul and Val Allison, Peter and Sue of Pete's Place, Ann Hubbard, Mrs Liddie Mann, Mr R. Kelly, Mr and Mrs John Allen and Richard Morling.

Sincerest thanks to Pam Graystone for allowing me to use her father's photographs, and to Ken Carsey for the use of his photographs and for information about his time at Richards' shipyard. Ken is one of the unsung photographers of the town, his photographs of Richards' are a valuable record of one of Lowestoft's great shipyards. Thanks to David Mackley for the use of one of his photographs and who also showed me around a surviving example of the Lowestoft tram shown in the frontispiece on page 4.

Thanks also to the Lowestoft branch of the Suffolk Record Office, in particular to Ruth, Emma, Brenda, Bill, Kelly and Ivan for their help and kindness. Others who have been of great help to me include the late Jack Rose, members of the Jack Rose Old Lowestoft Society, the Lowestoft Heritage Workshop Centre – in particular to Mark Thurgar for information about the town's MPs, Bob Collis and Robert Jarvis of the Lowestoft War Memorial Museum.

A sincere debt of gratitude goes to two great friends and associates who regretfully are no longer with us and who were of the greatest help and assistance to me over the years – John Rolph, antiquarian book-dealer, who died in the summer of 2006, and to Joan Plant, the youngest daughter of the Lowestoft photographer Christopher Wilson, who died at the grand old age of ninety-one in October 2008. To these two colleagues I dedicate this book.

All other material comes from my archive, therefore I would like to acknowledge, as always, a final debt of gratitude to all those photographers, amateur and professional, known and unknown, without whom this book could not be written.